# Twelve Films about Love and Heaven

## Other Books of Interest from St. Augustine's Press

# Twelve Films about Love and Heaven

PETER FRASER

ST. AUGUSTINE'S PRESS
South Bend, Indiana

Manufactured in the United States of America.

1 2 3 4 5 6 28 27 26 25 24 23

**Library of Congress Control Number: 2023935440**

Paperback ISBN: 978-1-58731-902-0
Ebook ISBN: 978-1-58731-903-7

∞ The paper used in this publication meets the minimum requirements of the American National Standard for Information Sciences – Permanence of Paper for Printed Materials, ANSI Z39.48-1984.

St. Augustine's Press
www.staugustine.net

To Martha
*Ego amo te*

## Table of Contents

# INTRODUCTION

> *AND therefore I pray thee, lean listily to this meek stirring of love in thine heart, and follow thereafter: for it will be thy guide in this life and bring thee to bliss in the tother. It is the substance of all good living, and without it no good work may be begun nor ended. It is nought else but a good and an according will unto God, and a manner of well-pleasedness and a gladness that thou feelest in thy will of all that He doth.*
>
> —The Cloud of Unknowing

I don't cry, Norman. This from Jesse Burns, the romantic interest in Robert Redford's *A River Runs Through It.* She speaks tilting her head slightly to the side while daubing an eye the way every girl knows to do, grieving the tragedy of her would-be-actor brother's failed life. He is a self-absorbed womanizing fool, but she loves him still, despite it all.

Few can watch Redford's film and not feel a familiar throb in the throat just at that moment of the simple gesture of the grieving sister, and again later when Norman's own tragic brother is pronounced "beautiful" by their mournful father, an old man broken to the point where he cannot even look up to engage a response.

Aestheticians since the 1950s have been ruminating over the strange, almost magical power of film art and drawing conclusions about its source from the formal to the political. It is about the nature of the iconic signs. It is about subconscious desires. It is about the subtle reinforcement of favorable power relationships. Meanwhile ordinary filmgoers have continued to react on the practical level, and if asked they would likely place the answer in a context more tangible; namely, the way film so readily taps into the tender realm of personal losses and longings.

Common after all is how we brush our griefs into soft piles out of sight, protecting ourselves from even the remembrance of the myriad losses we accumulate throughout the unleaving golden-grove of our lives, hoping that some movement in real time or in the measured-out time of art will not awaken the breeze to stir them back over the path. We are vulnerable and want solace but are troubled by the truth-telling balladeer,

*In every heart there is a room*
*A sanctuary safe and strong*
*To heal the wounds from lovers past*
*Until a new one comes along.*

That has been my experience. "I don't cry, Norman" could be our family motto, the heritage left by a gristled Scot stonemason grandfather who came to the new world with ten children and then promptly lost their mother and married again, and whose second wife, a good Irish woman, raised as many of the ten that she could recover from foster homes and then bore three of her own, two of whom received orders of the Church. And comingled with this inheritance of blood comes the solidity of the bungalows of Chicago at a time when John Wayne was the symbol of true manhood. Boys in our neighborhood readily believed that when your arm was shot off storming the beach at Normandy, you stooped down, picked it up, and kept moving. Men were taught to keep the faucet of the emotions tightly shut and do what must be done. Leave that maudlin business to the poor woman who will need your steady shoulder to guide her back into the house some dark day when pestilence or the angel of death visits.

Yet, I still cry along with Jesse every time. The film triggers something that the strongest efforts cannot hold back.

The art of film is so reliable a means, blending form with desire and our sense of physical smallness in a uniquely powerful way. An old, torn album with the faded photographs of our childhood home and the boy smiling from the top step of the porch in ill-fitting clothes may carry us into an afternoon reverie and drop us down moodily at the dinner table; but capture those images on celluloid and project them on the magic screen with wistful music in the elaborate illusion of a deft master, and something still more profound occurs.

The power in Redford's cinematic retelling of Norman Maclean's tragic novella lies in the magic medium exposing something pulsing quietly within us. That pulse touched and we feel suddenly and forcefully that though alive we are so very temporary, separated forever from the me that is gone forever, the lyrical, fading "young and easy" of Dylan Thomas,

*Oh as I was young and easy in the mercy of his means,*
*Time held me green and dying*
*Though I sang in my chains like the sea.*

The emotional effect of certain films emanates from their intrinsic beauty born from the complex graces of this quintessential art form capable of sculpting time and capturing the delicate nuances of life. That beauty is itself sourced in numinous realities bound together with the roots of our common humanity. Those realities combine two elements—*a longing to be fully known and a longing for permanence.* Call them *love and heaven.*

As human beings we desire, perhaps more than anything else, to have the narrative of our lives affirmed. We want to believe that we play a unique part in a master story in some ancient book with beginning, middle, and end. In that book surely a line can be drawn that curves unbroken through the arc of our lonely days. *My life starts here, right in this place and in this spot of time, and see how it glides upward, then falls again right there. See the loveliness of the slope and then those jagged ridges where it fell first, and again.* That story must exist; all our instincts attest that it must, and that story must stretch before and beyond us and touch both horizons of a world imagined with "the birth of the simple light/In the first, spinning place." We perceive that we have been loved into existence in a moment in time, for we are nourished in the deepest places only by love. And so, yes, we are or were known; to be loved and to be known are the same. We long for the old embraces which exist still in the mind as does the affection that warmed them, the comforts we felt from those who suffered alongside and who dared to confirm in word and gesture, if only a moment's glint of an eye, that we were and are real; and if real, then made for something even more real, something to come and permanent. Solid as a table yet fluid as no table can be. Heaven.

In 1914 Clive Bell wrote that "the starting point for all systems of aesthetics must be the personal experience of a peculiar emotion."[1] Art worth the name should move us in a peculiar way. Leo Tolstoy, though an aesthetician of a much different orientation, concurred with this point, "There is one indubitable indication distinguishing real art from its counterfeit, namely, the infectiousness of art."[2]

The two writers, opposite poles in aesthetic theory, had in view a core truth, the peculiar feeling drawn from us by all significant works of art. The art moves us because it is beautiful, but also because it touches us in a personal way, and it does so because of how we are designed. Bell, speaking along with his Bloomsbury modernists, developed his aesthetic principle to place emphasis on the formal elements that trigger the aesthetic emotion, what he called the "significant form" of great works, a form comprised of "lines and colours combined in a particular way" that "stir our aesthetic emotions." Tolstoy, the Christian romantic speaking alongside Tennyson and Hopkins and MacDonald and other aging knights of the former kingdom, likewise celebrated those forms of beauty, but sought to direct aesthetic analysis toward extrinsic principles, categories of honor and nobility and devotion and benevolence.

In this book, I will consider both but lean toward the latter; that is, the way the aesthetic beauty of a film evokes external categories of beauty that arouse bittersweet inner realities of the heart. Our interest will be less on the specific categories formed in the mind than on the experience of those longings in the heart, and what those experiences suggest; and by "heart" I mean an aspect of soul, the substance which creates our emotional responses, not the responses themselves. The art which moves us most deeply taps most deeply into the tender tendencies that define us as human. We long for love, and we long for heaven, for we sense we are made for both. We weep in those dearest moments of a film because we have lost hold of elements of our own time. In fact, we have lost and lost again and fear losing even more.

Though this analysis will, therefore, incline toward the metaphysical, the arguments will be more definite than would come from a purely aesthetic analysis of beauty. It is easier to identify the experiences a work of art brings us to recall and that move us than it is to explain why one work of art brings those experiences into sharper relief than another.

Harder yet are the levels of beauty achieved between kinds of art, say, painting versus music versus theater versus film. The influence of the film version of *A River Runs Through It* differs from that of Norman Maclean's source novel, which is why conversations about the merits or demerits of a novel to film adaptation so often seem tedious. Nonetheless, the "significant form" that moves us in such a film seems a question worth addressing, and it will be in a chapter to follow. Film like all art functions as vehicle of expression regarding truth in ways unavailable to complementary forms of art, and those vehicles of expression must be described if we are to talk at all about why this something is beautiful and why it means what it does.

The essays in this collection are also, of course, grounded in my personal experiences with certain films. After all, our "personal experience of a particular emotion" derives in large part from the tender points of our own losses; yet most readers will readily identify with them. The analyses will trace the form of each film to describe the internal system that becomes the film's beautiful language of evocation—its narrative structure, thematic arrangement, elements of style. Then the analyses will take the second logical step and address the relationship between the form of the work and the larger world of forms beyond it, those that warm the heart and light up the path which ends in our mysterious longing for divine love and heaven.

It is simpler to capture all this by using the terms associated with religious matters: when a film achieves a formal beauty, it incarnates a type of mystery, and the concomitant realization in we the viewer provokes something analogous to a mystical vision. We are awakened by the art to our immortality and to intimations of the divine power that birthed us in time and for time. Thus, broken free from cultural and temperamental restraints we have no recourse but to respond in an elevated way, our words too elusive to express well our thoughts. With inarticulate groanings we tell of our lost loves and hope that they likewise grieve our absence; we respond in tears the way we may shudder in the presence of a ghost in the house.

The unseen but sensed nonetheless, believed even while others deny—call it heaven. It may very well come through an echo from the laughter of the children in a distant place still ringing across the sky of our present in an old song. Or perhaps the laughter of lovers on the porches of our dream mansions conjured through the mist of pure imagination. If a certain slant of light oppressed the poet Emily Dickinson on winter afternoons, these slants of light from that other realm stir our hope contrariwise. Jessie Burns would not cry in front of Norman McLean if it were not that she knows what ought to be; that is, what her brother was meant to be, and perhaps what grace working through extreme suffering may yet bring him to be. The hope of heaven. Jessie's brother is our brother or father or self, and perhaps we will one day meet.

The Catholic philosopher Dietrich von Hildebrand drew a distinction between an association triggered in us through the "beautiful" and the way "our heart is touched by it."[3] Beauty "goes beyond this, since it awakens in our soul something that exists in a personal manner, something with a specifically affective nature." In our context the perfection of design, the significant form, of a masterful work of cinema like *A River Runs through It* captures in its beauty an experience common to all and deeply affecting, one which draws the curtain from our mortal experience to our secret selves. We respond without words, through a sudden mood. Call that mood joy as C. S. Lewis might or sorrow as Wordsworth might or melancholy as might Keats. It affects different souls differently. However, the source of the experience is the same for all. We long for love and live in a world where love is transitory, and we are made for heavenly permanence in a world slowly folding in upon itself.

What follows then are reflective essays on twelve twentieth-century films that have proven to stir the heart. I arranged the films initially in a chronological fashion with one film from each decade beginning with F.W. Murnau's *Sunrise* (1927) to Martha Fiennes' *Onegin* (1999). However, since the steam that drives the engine of the moving picture propels its subject toward greater and greater verisimilitude[4] and since that insistence produces a bias with most viewers to favor films more modern, it seemed best to work with the elements and reorganize the list from more recent films to older. Beyond this, it seemed likewise prudent to make a strong first step into the argument, and so the collection begins with a different film from the 1990s, Roberto Benigni's *Life Is Beautiful* (1998), as Benigni's film poses an artistic anomaly striking in effect which illustrates the point; that is, *Life Is Beautiful* is a perfect little film on a contrary topic that can only be fully understood in the context of the human experience these essays explore.

Should some readers disagree with the premises drawn here, perhaps compensation will come at least from a detailed examination of twelve works of ingenuity and beauty, which, whatever one concludes about the metaphysical realities behind them, make us feel glad to be alive. Some readers will no doubt quibble about the choices and prefer *Seventh Heaven*

(1927) to *Sunrise* or *Field of Dreams* (1989) to *The Natural* (1984). Such are always welcome to form their own lists and write their own books—the worst that can come from reasonable conflicts of taste and judgment will be, after all, the opportunity to enjoy two masterpieces and not just one, the "doubling of pleasures," as the Bard once upon a time suggested.

For the sake of categorical consistency, nearly all the films described in these pages can be classified as comedies, forms designed around the marriage bed and not the grave, despite how the graveyard embraces the shadow of the church tower and its bells. And so, for example, although *Life Is Beautiful* has been compared by those paid to render such judgments to *Saving Private Ryan* (1998) and *Open City* (1945) as all are about the horrors of the Second World War, the Benigni film addresses marriage principally, whereas the Spielberg and Rossellini films begin and end with meditations on death. The sorrow which waters the soil over those forever lost to time and memory has a different source, and so needs a different description.

The type of comedy that these films represent is the kind Western culture's greatest comic author, Dante, had in mind, the redemptive story of a world governed by benevolent providence with kind intentions toward the little souls seeking respite from the neverland of threat and misstep. Dante, after all, might have been lost forever in the dark wood but for the love of his Beatrice and her intercession for him with the Queen of Heaven, a grace in a world built and redeemed only by grace.

Finally, I selected the films in this volume with an eye for the non-politics of true diversity; in other words, the list is as international as could be without drifting down a path that might seem obscure or pedantic. So, while emphasis is placed on more familiar classics of American mythos like Robert Mulligan's *To Kill a Mockingbird* (1962), the scale is counterweighted with a classic film from a foreign, yet similar spring, Gabriel Axel's Danish masterpiece *Babette's Feast* (1987). The chronological structuring of the list allowed for the happy balance of something old, something new, something foreign, something....

The twentieth century which produced these films might well be described as the most violent and calamitous of human history. Our grandparents, entrusted with the task of preserving the Western culture so long crafted by the old guildsmen working under the towers of Christendom, fell into disarray under dark clouds of social transition and threat, clouds which hid their true enemies, who then led our parents off the cliff of the First World War. The bereft children fell into excess and despair where there should have been *jouissance.* Mercifully, the matter of human life has not fundamentally changed though the trajectory of Western culture has taken so drastic a downturn. The sun still rises brilliant in the still of the morning, and the birds welcome it with song, and the heart still longs for the consolations of human and divine love and sympathy, around the corner just ahead.

# 1

# LIFE IS BEAUTIFUL

*Nothing is sweeter than love, nothing stronger or higher or wider, nothing is more pleasant, nothing fuller, and nothing better in heaven or on earth, for love is born of God and cannot rest except in God, Who is created above all things.*

—Thomas à Kempis, The Imitation of Christ

Roberto Benigni's 1998 masterpiece *Life Is Beautiful* is a comedy set upon the backdrop of fascist Italy in the darkest period of that country's complicity with the genocidal campaign of the Third Reich, a period Italian historians and most ordinary Italians have worked to forget. Taking the cue from the awful contradictions of the times, the film presents a paradox: a comedy yet one wherein the groom father dies off-screen from a machine-gun blast in the back; and one in which the principal marriage is celebrated off-screen. Likewise, the film strays from narrative conventions, concluding in a freeze-frame with a voiceover introduced for the first time at the climactic moment of restoration between a widow and her orphan son.

In one of the more memorable scenes from *Life Is Beautiful,* the father, Guido, tries to shelter his son, Giosué, from the brutality of the prison camp where they have been sent as Jews by translating incorrectly the brutal orders of the German commander in charge. The three basic orders given are don't try to escape, don't ask questions just obey, and don't try to riot unless you want to be hung. Guido turns this into a child's game for Giosué wherein the child will lose points for crying, begging for his mother, or for a snack. It is a storyline impossible to explain adequately to anyone who has not seen the film; yet it works in a strange, magical way in context. The innocence of youth, the purity of the virgin, remains preserved in the bleakest of circumstances through the unlikeliest and kindliest of means.

Central to the scene is the governing motif of the whole endeavor—

the cruelty of the tyrant insisting on oppressive rules versus the father's pure and powerful desire that his son retain his green and golden vision of life, and the magic power of familial love. The tyrant has no happiness, no joy. The father has only his love and loyalty. The tyrant thinks life base and demands conditions to support whatever his personal happiness requires; the father thinks life beautiful and wants to be left alone to bask in its treasures with his young son.

Therein rests the argument—life is beautiful for those whose vision remains holy. Or perhaps, God stands behind the knight who martyrs himself to protect the children. The message describes the straightforward revelation the Gospel brought to light: *Blessed are the pure in heart for they shall see God.* Life is designed to be lived through the understanding of the consummation of all things, defined as a marriage celebration between the Savior and his bride. Jesus' first miracle converted jars of water into the best of wine so that ordinary people might celebrate community for at least one evening without the ugly intrusion of human corruption and failure.

Guido the protagonist has found the principal object of love in a woman, his dear Dora. She is a schoolteacher in a small town engaged fairy-tale style to a boorish local official and so doomed to a life locked in a tower. Guido finds her by chance while on a madcap adventure with a friend and is immediately smitten. He then courts her in the fashion of a poor but quixotic adventurer, even riding into her wedding dinner on a horse to steal her away at the last moment from the boor to whom she is betrothed. Guido and Dora marry and begin life in his maître d' uncle Eliseo's eclectic home and are blessed with a child and so offered an opportunity to pour all their love and creativity into the beauty of that new life, the boy Giosué.

The Christian overtones of the film could hardly be more evident, and especially coming from Benigni who went on from this film success to perform the poetry of Dante's *Comedia* in a one-man show "TuttoDante" that brought him international acclaim. Guido, the father, stands in type as the Christ. His wife, Dora, is Beatrice, the rescued mother of the living and the Blessed Mother as well. She gives to the world, not Guido, but something beautiful and new, Giosué. Guido will eventually give Giosué back to Dora by sacrificing his life in the camp, which is the other end of the world, the corrupt, dying side.

*Life Is Beautiful* was criticized when first released and seems to have been placed under a secret ban of silence by many in the critical elite, with only a few voices speaking as to how it might be considered an interesting case study for this or that scholarly context, as an example of historical revisionism in the 1990s, the rediscovery of the memoir as artifact, the new interest in Italian pro-fascist expressions during the war, the marketing of the Holocaust by the West, etc. The general attitude, initiated by certain prominent critics who objected to the paradoxical content upon the film's release, seems to be that when speaking about the Holocaust one is not allowed to say what Benigni says; namely, that life is holy and to be celebrated in all circumstances. The Holocaust is for the guardians of the modern cultural narrative a permanent emblem of the brutishness of the human enterprise taken as a whole, a topic that only certain people may speak about according to certain provisional assumptions and to advance very specific ideological ends. *The Guardian* ran an article after the film won its Academy Awards entitled "Does this Man Really Think the Holocaust Was a Big Joke?"[5] Such *ad hominem* attacks have come to be expected in our modern times. Five years later Mel Gibson's *The Passion of the Christ* (2004) would be criticized for making his depiction of the scourging and crucifixion of Christ too bloody, and Gibson would be labeled a hate-mongerer for his too accurate portrayal of the historical facts.

Benigni's *Life Is Beautiful* places the horror of the genocide within a theological context, making the story a somewhat farcical morality play illustrating familial love against the demonic, a creative endeavor reminiscent of C. S. Lewis' equally arresting *Screwtape Letters.* Benigni's subject is not specifically a proper attitude toward the Holocaust, but the beauty and holiness and wonder of all life as defined in the old faith. One might see the statement as the antithesis of something like Shusaku Endo's dark novel *Silence.*

Despite the judgments of the professional critical class, truth always draws followers, or they are drawn by it. And *Life Is Beautiful* did become an international sensation when released and won numerous awards simply because of the power it exercised over film audiences. In many theaters, as was the case when my wife and I first saw it in Milwaukee upon its release, the audience stood and cheered at its conclusion, many of us with eyes still wet from crying through the bittersweet resolution. No doubt some measure of that effect will continue whenever it is seen, though chances are the film will not show up at university film symposiums or in art houses anytime soon, unless in the context of what historians and artists ought and ought not say or do.

The singular cause of the infectious response from ordinary viewers of *Life Is Beautiful* would seem to be its rendering of patriarchal love, and patriarchal love in the divine ideal. Guido the father gives his life not just to keep Giosué alive, but also to keep Giosué in love with life. Along with that, Guido the father is lover/husband who rescues and redeems Dora, whose life until his entrance seems destined for misery and disillusion.

The film might be best measured by applying the author's love for the greatest of Christian poets: *Life Is Beautiful* is a divine comedy composed and performed by a comic, Benigni, who has spent a large portion of his professional life immersed in Dante. It begins not with the hero blocked from Mt. Joy by the beasts of incontinence, murder, and intrigue, but with the hero wandering without an object through a world under the boot of fascism and diabolism. In the opening scene Guido and his poet friend Ferruccio drive the Italian countryside en route to some city where the friend has lined up steady work as an upholsterer. Guido, whose craft is less defined than Ferruccio—he will obtain work as a waiter—seems to have no aim except to settle into a life where he can direct his seemingly infinite capacity for affection. After the brakes fail, their car careens through a thicket and then a village until it settles on the grounds of a small farm. There Guido will introduce himself to a young girl standing by as Prince Guido and catch his princess, Dora, who just happens at that moment to fall from a hay loft.

Smitten at first meeting with this princess who fell from the sky, Guido's elaborately contrived courtship of Dora follows. He finds her at a theater watching *Tales of Hoffmann* and stares at her through the barcarolle as she sits unaware in her balcony seat until she feels his gaze and turns her head toward him. He then shows up at her school and delights the bored children awaiting the fascist school inspector. Later he transforms a car into a chariot to save her from the rain and the boorish fiancé. He delights her with his cleverness and simple attention and tells her at the gate of her home that he desires more than anything else to make love to her again and again. Guido then completes the courtship by rescuing Dora at the engagement party and riding her off on a fairytale horse, or so his imagination makes it. When they arrive at the uncle's house where Guido is staying, it is the

rescued bride Dora who then leads him into the conservatory to consummate their love among the flowers. The sequence ends cleverly with Giosué leading Guido out of the conservatory some years later.

Guido's love affair with Dora presents a fairy tale within a film that affirms the belief in fairy tales as the nearest conceptions we have apart from direct revelation of the possibilities for heaven conceived from earth. Each time Guido greets Dora with "*Buongiorno, Principessa,*" he waters the flower of fairyland love, that love whose origin is divine and whose working capricious. Chesterton would nod his approval. Puck has anointed Guido's eyes. Dora is a princess to be loved despite the realities of her circumstances—her father is absent, her mother is a Nazi sympathizer, her fiancé is a vindictive and corrupt bureaucrat, she is a bored teacher in a miserable government school, and her temper is at times petulant. All these things tell against his love, but Guido still loves, and his love redeems this captured maiden. When he and Giosué and Eliseo are arrested to be deported by car and then train to Auschwitz, Dora insists on getting on the death train with them. She is no longer the Dora we met at the start of the film. She has been translated into the Dora of Guido's and Dante's imagination.

Before continuing along this line, it is necessary to step to the side and address the cynical modern critic who insists that the fairytale love that joins Guido and Dora is the very thing which makes the film implausible and unrealistic. For the modern thinker, reality means something rooted in causality, while the type of behavior the film celebrates is conventional and old-fashioned, fanciful not real, and, therefore, not good art; so goes their thinking. That false logic must be challenged if only because it spells the death of so much of beauty which ordinary mortals have celebrated in poetry and song, and frankly lived for. The best response to the modern critic is to borrow directly from Chesterton, the twentieth century's greatest apologist of fairyland, who in his conversion story *Orthodoxy* argues that the seeming monotony and predictability of a thing like human courtship might instead be an argument for the intrinsic goodness and beauty of the thing, not its mundanity. Beauty is chosen repeatedly because it provides such repeated joy:

> *All the towering materialism which dominates the modern mind rests ultimately upon one assumption; a false assumption. It is supposed that if a thing goes on repeating itself it is probably dead; a*

> *piece of clockwork. People feel that if the universe was personal it would vary; if the sun were alive it would dance. This is a fallacy even in relation to known fact. For the variation in human affairs is generally brought into them, not by life, but by death; by the dying down or breaking off of their strength or desire... The sun rises every morning. I do not rise every morning; but the variation is due not to my activity, but to my inaction. Now, to put the matter in a popular phrase, it might be true that the sun rises regularly because he never gets tired of rising. His routine might be due, not to a lifelessness, but to a rush of life. The thing I mean can be seen, for instance, in children, ... They always say, "Do it again"; and the grown-up person does it again until he is nearly dead. For grown-up people are not strong enough to exult in monotony. But perhaps God is strong enough to exult in monotony. It is possible that God says every morning, "Do it again" to the sun; and every evening, "Do it again" to the moon. It may not be automatic necessity that makes all daisies alike; it may be that God makes every daisy separately, but has never got tired of making them.*[6]

The courtship and conquest of lover and beloved and their consummation in the conservatory prompt the first moments of genuine elevation in the film. Guido has demonstrated to and through Dora the transformative power of devotion and drawn out of her something entirely new and exalted. In sanctifying his object, he is likewise raised to the heroic potential the second part of the film will demonstrate. And we are drawn in to watch and celebrate.

There is a special moment in Shakespeare's great tragedy *King Lear*, when Lear awakens from his illness and dementia to the loving gaze of his wronged, banished daughter Cordelia and asks whether such dreams are possible.

> *I fear I am not in my perfect mind.*
> *Methinks I should know you, and know this man;*
> *Yet I am doubtful; for I am mainly ignorant*
> *What place this is; and all the skill I have*
> *Remembers not these garments; nor I know not*

*Where I did lodge last night. Do not laugh at me;*
*For (as I am a man) I think this lady*
*To be my child Cordelia.*

After Cordelia offers her forgiveness and love, he repents of all, "You must bear with me./Pray you now, forget and forgive. I am old and foolish" (IV.7). It is a scene one imagines must have caused Shakespeare to weep. And so here. Guido's love has beatified the beloved and the child they will produce. All the past is washed away, and to the point where Dora can walk with Guido into the hellish camp with the firmness of a martyr.

At the heart of the divine comedy of the old faith is divine love. Dante loved Beatrice, so when he is lost and languishing in the dark wood, she petitions heaven on his behalf and is allowed an audience with Claire the saint who grants clarity of vision and to Mary who provides access to her Son. Virgil is then sent from heaven to lead the pilgrim poet from his spiritual death to the place of holy vision that completes the *Paradiso*. Guido has loved his Dora, and she has found her life in his love.

When the two interact at the prison camp, it is entirely in this new fairyland context, and we see this repeated three times. The first will be when Guido finds a microphone left open in an empty office and calls Dora with the familiar *Buongiorno, Principessa* and reminds her of his love and that Giosué is safe. We see the effect in her eyes as she steps forward from the huddle of other imprisoned women to listen. The second comes when he finds a phonograph left in a room at the dining hall where he has been allowed to serve the officers and their children. He turns the horn to the window and plays loud the Offenbach aria that played when he first beheld Dora in the balcony during the opera. Again, we see the effect in her face lifted in the classical pose of the Madonna looking toward heaven as she receives her husband's loving message. The third time will be as Guido searches the camp for Dora to warn her not to get into the trucks heading for the gas chamber prior to the abandonment of the camp. In this scene his message will not reach her until after his martyrdom when Giosué will find her in the line of women leaving the camp and tell her how his papa won the game for him.

Each of these scenes is moving beyond words. Still the cinematography is not exceptional; the acting is convincing but understated; the dialog is spare. No tricks are performed to evoke so powerful a response in the viewer beyond the reaction shots of Dora in the first two scenes. In the third scene, mother and child embrace and fall to the ground, but then the shot freezes with neither looking in the direction of the camera.

So, what provokes the powerful response? It is worthwhile to examine the phonograph scene more closely for an answer. Guido has been granted an opportunity to play waiter to a dinner for the officer's children at the camp and has smuggled Giosué into the event. Afterwards as he cleans up, he notices the phonograph on a table near a window and then finds the Offenbach aria among the records lying beside. The scene begins devoid of any dialog, allowing only the soft ambient sounds of the phonograph arm and needle and then the sound of the music. Guido opens the window and turns the phonograph horn toward it, and the camera then fancifully carries the music to and through the window of the women's barracks where Dora is held. We see the bodies of the sleeping women and then Dora who emerges from her bed, called by the love song. She moves to the window and the camera studies her face as the music speaks to her of Guido's love,

*Time flies by, and carries away*
*our tender caresses for ever!*
*Time flies far from this happy oasis*
*and does not return.*

*Burning zephyrs,*
*embrace us with your caresses!*
*Burning zephyrs,*
*give us your kisses! Your kisses! Your kisses!*

*Ah! Lovely night, oh night of love, smile upon our joys!*
*Night much sweeter than the day,*
*oh beautiful night of love! Ah!*
*Smile upon our joys!*
*Night of love, oh night of love!*

Dora's face is the end point of the composition, a canvas for the love which plays over her. The camera techniques make plain the subject. Yet, in this scene the plot is not significantly advanced, nor is the theme a new element in the story. Rather, like Hebrew poetry, the theme has just been amplified in the moment, made more intimate because all other story elements are enhanced. What remains is as strong as ever and more so for its poignancy. Benigni allows one crosscut showing Guido's courteous attitude as he smiles knowing the effect of the song. But the subject is the reception by Dora of her husband's gift. In the grimmest of circumstances, as Guido will most certainly be killed, love speaks to the heart that this world is not all there is. The intensity of the horror around the two simply makes their devotion more powerful and moving and permanent. And this is the only viable explanation for the response this scene draws from the viewer. The barcarolle is not just for Dora, but for us, and it comes not just from the mind of the father and lover hero, but from a source beyond the mortal coil we will one day shuffle off. It passes through Dora to us. Guido's act is an emblem of the power beyond ordinary experience that invests all such inventions of love, and that enlivens and ennobles all created things, "a source sublime," as Wordsworth put it; the love of the Father and the Son and as expressed through all creation, and particularly and peculiarly in the bond between man and woman, as Dante saw it.

Parallel to this demonstration of sublimity between the man and the woman, a love discrete while honest, passionate while restrained, comes the secondary romance of *Life Is Beautiful*, the relationship between Guido and Giosué. The voice-over that concludes the film states, "This is my story. This is the sacrifice my father made. This was his gift to me." Guido has been compelled to play father and mother to his son through the camp experience, performing slave labor in the factory and constantly on the alert to protect Giosué from capture by the guards and guard dogs, a miracle he accomplishes through a slate of creative means. As he is marched off to his death, he wears a makeshift scarf and skirt he put on earlier in the story to look for Dora in the women's quarters. Giosué watches him from inside a storage box, his limited vision through its opening a metaphor for the protection of innocence Guido has provided. Guido looks toward the box as he passes, and in a final gesture that makes permanent in memory his sacrifice, he plays at high stepping to a mock trial, while marching to the real one awaiting him in the alley. The concluding voiceover suggests that Giosué in time has come to understand the depth of his father's understanding, and how love can produce a clarity about the "things that are not" that overcome "the things that are," to borrow from the language of St. Paul.

Guido is by no means a perfect man. He plays at life and has a naïve understanding of the potential not only of human evil, but the infinite human capacity for the denial of complicity in that evil. He plays a riddle game with the hotel guest in his Italian town, Dr. Lessing, and when that same man shows up as chief medical officer at the death camp, Guido naively thinks he may be willing to help Guido and his family escape. The viewer has recognized sooner that Lessing has separated himself from sanity and entered an imaginary world of riddles to keep from the realization of the barbarities of his duties. Guido is no deep thinker. His companion Ferruccio is the poet and reader of Schopenhauer. Guido will take Ferruccio's lesson about Schopenhauer's concept of the mastery of the will as a kind of magic wand and use it to attempt a spell on Dora at the opera and later the guard dog that threatens to expose Giosué in his final hiding place in the camp.

These lighthearted moments underscore the simple nature of the hero—he is common, but pure. Guido is an ordinary man who for reasons not offered in this fairy tale enters the plot with the intention to place his love upon an ordinary object. He is quixotic, yet not truly mad—his is a genuine devotion that sees the world and his maiden truthfully and who evokes a genuine response. In exercising true virtue and persisting against all common reason, he transforms his world and the objects of his love. He stands as the emblem of Everyman, but not the one who must find the path for himself to the gates of heaven, rather the Everyman who finds his best end by making it his vocation to see others to and through those gates. And in this role, he stands for something else, too, which is perhaps the highest longing of every human heart: Guido stands for the devoted father and spouse whose life takes its final perfect shape in martyrdom.

An interesting cross-reference to the story of *Life Is Beautiful* is Corrie Ten Boom's *The Hiding Place*, a Holocaust memoir that was made into a modestly successful film in 1975. The Ten Boom family had been hiding Jews in their Haarlem home in the Netherlands until discovered and carted off to a concentration camp in Scheveningen and then Vught. Not unlike the protagonist of Benigni's tale, Corrie spends much of her time at the camp supporting her saintly sister Betsy who busily tends to the women around her. Betsy has transformed even the women's flea-infested dorm into a place of blessing. Were it not for the fleas, Betsy concludes, the women would not have been able to get together to read the Bible that Betsy smuggled in, and the women would not be able to pray for one another's needs; the guards refused to enter such filthy quarters. So, one might say, life was beautiful in that dorm as well, although Betsy would die as ignominiously as does Guido. The success of the story told in *The Hiding Place* would likewise compel Corrie to the work she would do after the experience, traveling the world to share the hope that she carried away from those horrors. Both stories, the fiction told by Benigni and the memoir of Corrie Ten Boom, share the blending of the holy with the debased, and to redemptive ends. In this both look back to medieval sensibilities, where gargoyles were granted space alongside angels and saints. It is this paradoxical fusion so central to the older Christian faith that puzzles those who approach *Life Is Beautiful* with the tenets of modern despair written on machine-made paper held desperately in their tight fists.

Guido's martyrdom will allow the young Giosué to see the world as it needs to be seen. Rather than mastering the will through asceticism and art as Schopenhauer may have suggested, Guido masters the corruptions around him through true charity, and so provides his son a more hopeful path forward than philosophic pessimism. As the father has practiced, so the son will view the world as holy and will see in his own life a complete narrative with beginning, middle, and end, with heroes and villains, played in a forest that is unspeakably dangerous, yet altogether the proper setting to understand the sublime rule of God. That is the ultimate gift of the father and of this film.

In our post-Kantian world, to declare openly the sanctity of life is tantamount to heresy. Who knows what life is after all? Aesthetic truth makes existence only bearable according to modernist philosophy. Life is certainly not joyful, but brutish; thus, we need to escape through our fictions. We need the crutch of religion per Marx. Assertive force per Nietzsche. The governors say we need social control, population control, economic control, medical control—some enterprise of collective will. A drug or genetic modification will do perhaps, or both in one vial, anything to ease the psychological trauma of existence.

We say no; that is, all in all, taken in its entirety and even in the smallest particulars, life is mysterious and beautiful and holy, despite all, in the midst of all. To say such a thing is too certain and too old, and such speech rubs hard against the fibrous assumptions of modernity. The great enterprise of enlightenment progress must be allowed to press forward without resistance. We live in a wheezing civilization that has begun to grieve existence itself, and Lear-like must banish the seer to the storm. As Chesterton lamented a century ago:

*What will there be to remember*
*Of us in the days to be?*
*Whose faith was a trodden ember*
*And even our doubts not free...*

Of course, the people who press us toward the utopia wherein life will be made tolerable for the most sufferers possible, those people often strike us as the least happy. Perhaps they say they will be happy when more comply, but they never quite seem to get to that state of compliant contentment; always one more non-compliance erasure to be made. And as time passes and those erasures multiply, the unhappiness of the planners turns to barbaric inhumanity, and their despair becomes overwhelming all the while they feed upon the blood of the martyrs.

That said, what can never be erased from the world is beauty, for beauty ever discovers new ways to express itself. *Life Is Beautiful* makes this point so well—by direct statement and by way of illustration, for the film is a lovely thing. Dietrich von Hildebrand wrote, "There is first of all the value of the beauty itself, a specifically aesthetic value that adheres to the object."[7] In Benigni's masterpiece, truth and freshness breathe lovely through all the surprising devices. If it were not so, the effect would likely have been ridicule and not tears.

# 2
# ONEGIN

*The double grief of a lost bliss/Is to recall its happy hour in pain.*
*—Dante Alighieri,* The Inferno, Canto V

More an eighteenth-century rake than a true romantic, at least in his life and poetic attitudes, Lord Byron did bequeath to the generations of romantics to follow the form for a new hero, not a noble knight as in the medieval tradition, but a collapsed humanist. The Byronic hero is that character who like Byron himself perhaps in his campaign in Greece, and certainly like the wanderer of his early popular work *Childe Harold's Pilgrimage*, shares a destiny with the poets and philosophers trapped forever in the grey bower within the Inferno, a character of noble potential tormented by what he knows he has lost and can never recover. Call it lost innocence or moral paralysis or failed love, attribute it to a dead paramour as in Poe or lost potency as in Hemingway, the Byronic hero is trapped in a hell of regret and self-absorption with no means of return or restoration.

This Byronic hero found a distinct shape in the masterpiece verse novel of Byron's contemporary, the Russian poet Alexander Pushkin. Pushkin's *Eugene Onegin* was written over a period of eight years from May of 1823 through October of 1831 while the great Russian poet traveled between various provincial estates outside Moscow and Petersburg. It is the story of a dissolute young gentleman who at a point of acute world-weariness travels to the country from St. Petersburg upon hearing he has inherited an estate from his uncle. While there in semi-exile, he meets the Larens family, a widow and two young daughters, Olga and Tatyana, provincials from the neighboring estate Krasnogórie. Olga is betrothed to Lenski, a young man of modest poetic and social talents, whom Onegin befriends. The beautiful and enigmatic sister Tatyana, on the other hand, becomes the immediate object of the exiled gentleman. Onegin, who is rather a snob in the Pushkin novel, "an exemplary pupil of fashions," manages to offend the sensitive Lenski by suggesting his poetic gifts not worth exploring and his darling Olga rather ordinary. This results in a duel and Lenski's execution—Onegin being more practiced. Prior to that calamity, Tatyana, who has barely spoken to Onegin but asked him for books and observed him from afar as the thing itself of culture and refinement, has written him a passionate letter of declaration, revealed late in the narrative as a masterpiece of sincerity and deep feeling. However, rather than recognize the letter and the girl's natural brilliance and accept her sincere and passionate offer, Onegin refuses Tatyana on the grounds that their romance would go the usual way toward boredom and infidelity. It is this act of folly that leads to the other, Onegin's petty attempt to seduce Lenski's Olga just to make his point, which provokes the disastrous duel.

The story then proceeds in fast-forward six years. Olga has gotten over Lenski and been betrothed to an army officer. Tatyana has been wed to an officer of higher rank and moved into palatial accommodations in Petersburg. Meanwhile Onegin has been wandering aimlessly, tortured by the consequences of his self-defeating choices. When by chance he meets the now aristocratic Tatyana at an elegant party, his interest is rekindled, and he pursues her only to find her integrity resolute. It is too late for such matters, she proclaims; she will remain faithful to her husband, love him or not. Onegin, broken and defeated, goes off to roam "o'er the earth."

The ironic narrative tone of Pushkin's novel muffles the effect of the disaster as the narrator has introduced Onegin as a character lacking genuine heroic attributes. He is a product of a father who "lived by means of debts" and a corrupt court culture, a young man whose only real gift was an early-formed ability to "disturb the hearts of the professed coquettes." As such, the novel crystalizes the character of the Byronic hero in a somewhat negative light, the way one could say Conan Doyle did by popularizing the fictional private eye idealized in the three original short stories of Edgar Alan Poe that introduced the genius romantic poet, C. Auguste Dupin. In doing so through the mediation of his very cool and objective narrator, Pushkin encourages his reader to place the story of Eugene Onegin in its larger context of the rural-bred Pushkin's distaste for upper-class society. Onegin's folly is a priggish inability to see the genuine beauty and poetic soul of Tatyana until forced to do so as result of his surprisingly profound sense of loss. When he pursues the woman in the last scenes, it is more an extension of his vanity since he does so with the corrupted understanding of the gentleman of court thinking marriage merely a convention of social order, not a sacrament of the heart. His intention must be to make her his concubine, one assumes, an outcome calling to mind the hopeless conclusion to Anton Chekhov's masterpiece short story, "The Lady with the Dog":

> *It seemed to them that fate had intended them for one another, and they could not understand why she should have a husband, and he a wife. They were like two migrating birds, the male and the female, who had been caught and put into separate cages.*

Readers might conclude from Pushkin that Onegin rather deserves what he gets, a better outcome than should he ruin Tatyana to satisfy his pride and passion. In the end, the narrator offers a moral to the story, that the reader "may find at least a crumb" of common sense about the real mystery of the human condition in his tale, and so recognize the threat that refined culture poses to our natural wonder, humility, and temporal happiness.

By the time Martha Fiennes took on the material to make her 1999 film version with her brother, Ralph Fiennes, playing the title character, the material had taken on a separate life as prototype within a larger literary conversation that had evolved throughout the nineteenth and twentieth centuries, and the subject in particular of a grand Tchaikovsky opera and a fine Soviet era film by Roman Tickhomirov. Both the opera and 1959 film steered the material away from the title character toward the more elusive and lyrical Tatyana. Fiennes took in this tradition but shifted back through it toward Onegin himself, making him even more tragic than had Pushkin—not a dissolute rake too full of his own success with women to see a real woman, but a poet corrupted by society and not willing to see the means of escape from that corruption when offered it by a woman of similar temperament. In other words, Fiennes keeps the perspective of the feminine, but the feminine observing and reacting to the object of desire; that is, Tatyana idealizing and then grieving the lost potential lover Onegin might have become.

*Onegin* is more tragic than the dark, beautifully composed anecdote of

Pushkin. To that end, Fiennes redeems Pushkin's cynical romanticism by restoring the deep old-world morality behind it. Her film offers an emphatic morality tale about how disordered love may lead from potential redemption to damnation; that is, the offer of redemption and the choice of damnation instead. One also might very well say the film accomplishes a minor miracle of artistic conception and execution by translating the brilliant Pushkin original poem into complementary, haunting visual lyricism.

Fiennes' Onegin is a soul caught in the balance who is provided two chances to save himself from a "grievous peril." The first chance comes as birthright of all mortals stepping into a world charged, as Hopkins put it, with the "glory of God." The camera constantly reminds the viewer that the rural environment the hero is sentenced to is not oppressive, but lovely and beckoning. Immersed, not sentenced, in its beautiful mysteries, Onegin is presented opportunity to embrace common grace and step through its sweet influence as had Wordsworth and Thoreau. But he will not. The second chance comes through providential revelation, when Tatyana presents to Onegin the letter declaring her love and then meets him privately in the hope of a response in kind. Her beauty and sincerity are as compelling as the landscape; but again, he refuses to yield. In those two telling moments, divine grace has knocked upon the door of his heart and is turned away.

The sequence that best depicts nature's offer of common grace is early and sets up the quarrel which will lead to the tragic duel. Shortly after Onegin arrives at his country estate, he engages Tatyana in his library and offers her Rousseau's novel *Heloise* to read. While exploring the room, she sees a set of his satirical portrayals of Petersburg society and declares that she "likes the country." He smiles softly and studies her, thus setting up the romantic connection that feeds the following quiet scene at the lake on Lenski's estate. Onegin is lying on the dock while Lenski tosses stones into the sparkling water. Nearby yet out of immediate sight, Tatyana has reclined in a boat like the lady in the famous Waterhouse painting. When a splash in the water attracts Tatyana's notice, she begins to study secretly the two men, and especially Onegin as he reclines on the dock in a languorous position that recalls another pre-Raphaelite painting, Wallis' "Death of Chatterton." For a moment Onegin feels Tatyana's gaze and all that it implies, but just then Lenski, who longs for his friend's approval, breaks the reverie by asking if Onegin will read one of his poems. The question is pregnant with significance, as acceptance of life in the country will mean for Onegin true charity, a concern for the real people who fill that country tableau. He is thus offered opportunity to accept the gift of Lenski's friendship and all the other simple gifts nature offers in this place, including the observing young girl who is opening her heart. All he need do is show some common courtesy, but, as if from an uncontrollable impulse, Onegin reverts to condescension, replying in a tone that suggests the divide of class and culture between the men is too great. This insult sets up the tragic events. The court-bred antihero has rebuked easy friendship, the countryside, and the young girl in the distance birthed and raised in its purer air.

The sequence that best portrays what might be termed Onegin's rejection of a more revelatory grace comes in an opposite setting, within the gazebo outside the Larens' home in the evening. It is the girl's name day and she and Onegin have played cat and mouse during the party. In that spirit, she exits to lure him to follow and meet her in a secret place. The gazebo is at the base of a fairyland hill, a remote spot where she no doubt expects they may consummate their love. She wears a white gown and the room is old and white, out of a girl's daydream. Onegin comes wearing his black suit and a top hat. Whereas Tatyana is timid and hopeful, Onegin, as in the scene with Lenski, reverts to the manner of the practiced courtier; he will be returning her love letter so that she will not be compromised. Tatyana prods him to give up the pose and be sincere, but the more she does the more he adopts the affected attitude of the distant rake who cannot love—love leads only to society, marriage, boredom, adultery. When he next begins to wax sentimental on her youth and prospects, she inquires if he indeed feels nothing. And in that climactic and damning moment he tells a lie, as becomes evident, and says no, to which she utters, "You curse yourself." Onegin registers that prophecy with a stare but walks back to the party to play at seducing Lenski's Olga, out of spite. So, here Onegin has been offered more than common grace, far more than the country life offered on its own. He has had placed before him an intimate gift from heaven, this young, innocent girl who will love and be devoted to him for life. In rejecting the gift, he indeed curses himself.

Tatyana offers a particular love, but she represents all friends, mothers, daughters, and lovers who call men back to that one hope for social redemption—marriage and family happiness. St. Paul wrote that women are saved through the bearing of children, making a reference back to Eve the mother of the living who would find her path to heaven through the bearing of her child, Christ, who would reverse the curse. In Christian tradition, mankind is thus rescued by the very woman who came bearing the forbidden fruit. She comes a second time bearing the redemptive fruit while accepting as penance the desire for the man who will rule over her despite his desperate need for her love and special gifts. In offering herself to Onegin, Tatyana offers redemption and passion, for she alone can lead him to a meaningful temporal life, and back to God. His fatuous terms of dismissal which they both recognize as such, closes the door on his opportunity for earth and heaven. When Onegin comes to her years later with a plea for pity and love, her response of "You are too late" addresses him as the damned soul he has made of himself, a soul who has resisted grace and so lost it forever, like Esau who wept for his sold birthright but could never get it back.

It is precisely his rejection of this very high offer of redemption, the pure woman offering herself body and soul to this one man, that gives the film *Onegin* its peculiar power. Just as films that render full dimensionality to stories of divine love and some momentary vision of heaven produce an ache and longing in the human heart, and tears, so this film produces a deep ache, not through our longing but through our fear of losing the precious object of the longing. This is the fear that Aristotle described but could only frame in materialist, categorical terms. Tragedy in the Christian tradition has a deeper metaphysical dimension, for it presents the final loss of heaven and the beatific vision. This Christian fear warns us to stay vigilant and keep waiting for grace to enter our cottage, hospitality being the epitome of human virtue and the way to receive the savior. Tatyana's "You are too late" recalls the parable of the ten virgins, "And while they were going to buy, the bridegroom came, and those who were ready went in with him to the marriage feast, and the door was shut. Afterward the other virgins came also, saying, 'Lord, lord, open to us.' But he answered, 'Truly, I say to you, I do not know you.'" A tragic parable designed to engender the beginning of wisdom.

The film's visual metaphor for this great loss is snow. Whereas many artists have suggested snow as an emblem of grace and beauty, Fiennes goes back to a more primary motif wherein snow suggests absence and death, the very opposite of the passion that produces love and life. We see this from the opening moments.

Onegin is seated in a carriage driven through the snow to the country estate for his uncle's funeral. He is slumped, huddled inside his furs, deeply engaged in internal self-loathing. When will the devil take me, he thinks, and the voice of his thought plays over scenes of the tedium and depravity of the society life he has departed. The images cut back to the straight-line journey through the bleak countryside enshrouded in white. Onegin is self-aware and able to identify the source of his despair, unlike the original Pushkin character who seems blindsided by the tragedy awaiting his future. In this film version, the antihero is also identified early as an artist who draws caricatures of societal depravity in an idiosyncratic style, as well as beautiful images; later we will see a haunting sketch he draws of but never personally shows the beautiful Tatyana. He is a man who knows what the good should be and that he has gone away from it, while he is also cynical and fatally enamored with his own ability to identify and castigate sham.

Such a start makes plain the nature of the problem. Onegin is not merely debauched, but spiritually dead by self-decree. He has chosen damnation from the start, the narrative beginning with him at a point of paradoxical hubris, "When will the devil take me." He seems to declare himself damned as a show of control. It is one thing to be depraved like a Dorian Gray and hide from that with veiled regret; it is quite another to fall in love with that same regret as a means of backhanded self-praise. Later in the story when Onegin in a cruel moment will tell Lenski that he is provincial and that his beloved Olga common, he does so with affected unconcern for how such a declaration might do damage, as though the necessity of revealing truth mitigates the duty to love neighbor and desire his good. It is this priggishness that enrages Lenski, and which Lenski then imitates in his own fashion when promoting the duel.

The snow has thus frosted over Onegin's heart. Ralph Fiennes conveys this skillfully through a consistently distant demeanor even when gazing unobserved at Tatyana. Only in the final scene in Tatyana's home in an all-white room with enormous height and little furniture do we see Onegin break into genuine emotion up close, but then, as said, it is too late.

This harsh end is presaged in the duel where the bullet travels toward Lenski in slow motion and strikes his forehead in close and full view, rendering the whole action especially cool and calculated. Onegin's heart intention is likewise communicated by the slow way he has dropped his pistol and aimed. It is an interesting alteration of the Pushkin original that Lenski fires first and misses, providing Onegin the opportunity to end the duel without bloodshed. In the original the more superficial Onegin fires as Lenski aims and before he can get off a shot. Fiennes' Onegin, as if compelled by demonic energy, executes his friend with the shot to the head, only to whisper "Vladimir" in his ear and sob over him after the fact. A disease of consummate pride has driven him to this fatal deed.

As backdrop to this duel enacted through an early morning fog is a windmill at the edge of the dock, its blade turning slowly with groaning insistence. The rotation of the blade is untrue, a fact brought to Lenski's attention at the start of the sequence by his pock-marked second, a cold agent of death in the flesh. The event and Onegin are likewise untrue. Tatyana watches the tragedy unfold from a distance and then races up a hill to let the other women of the house, and Olga in particular, know the terrible outcome. To capture her perspective, the ambient sounds are muted and replaced by the haunting melody of Magnus Fiennes' soundtrack, a device which heightens the tension to draw out the agony of those involved, while keeping the viewer some distance away. Onegin is likewise kept separate as fate's agent in the debacle, a victim used for this evil purpose and destined for dismissal.

In similar style in a later scene, the camera will tease Onegin to suggest the way deferred desire will now forever tease him. It comes when the doomed lover observes the now married Tatyana skating alone in Petersburg Square. As he stands on the rim of the ice rink watching her glide past, she returns his gaze with expressionless eyes. A female acquaintance of Onegin stumbles her way over to where he stands and begins chatting in the hope that he will come and skate with her, but Onegin remains hypnotized by the impassive Tatyana. As if placing a period at the sentence's end, Tatyana skates directly toward him before making one final arc and skating away, leaving him to his misery.

This last scene is witnessed with jealous interest by the husband, a cousin of Onegin, who clearly suspects trouble. Instead, that evening Tatyana comes to him in their bed in a hot passion reminiscent of the passion she suffered early in the story while writing the fated letter. She chooses in this moment to give her husband as duty the free gift Onegin had rejected, and in doing so she seems intent on reversing the spell cast by the previous, tragic and unfulfilled relationship. Hers is a curious act of marital charity born of deep suffering that offers context for the climactic scene when she will turn Onegin away for good.

Tatyana is never described in the film as an object of sexual desire for Onegin, despite her first appearance in the second part of the film dressed in a red gown. Romantic passion and sexual passion are separate matters, and Onegin seems to like keeping it that way, saving his sexual passions for his independent life in Petersburg. If sexual desire is aligned with any of the principal players at the country estate, it would be with Tatyana herself in her fever thinking of her dream lover and writing her invitation to love. Onegin's expressed feelings toward Tatyana remain of a higher order, as evidenced by his drawing of her with hair up in a classic style. She stands as poetic inspiration, as he will tell Lenski, and so is perhaps best kept at a distance. His first sight captures her as the remote beauty of the villages, as she walks through the town square her head covered in a scarf, a portrait worthy of Tolstoy in a story like *The Cossacks*. She exists to this Byronic antihero as something to be possessed but not really loved; and certainly not as what modern feminist critics term the "object of the male gaze." She exists for him to inspire high art not to be soiled, and certainly not by someone with his background. Of course, an attitude like Onegin's still turns people into things to be consumed and not real people with real feelings and independence; his is a sham view of the holy fed by ego, not love.

Critical to the impact of Pushkin's original and all significant remakes is the revelation about Tatyana, that she has all along been the consummate poet artist within a story where all the major players strive for that title in one way or another. Not only is she genuinely lovely and original and pure, but the beauty of her letter surpasses any language expressed by other characters. Pushkin, as mentioned, presents the content of the letter late in his poem, and it comes as a startling and refreshing counterpoint for the reader grown weary of the manner of his ironic narrator, as well as the protagonist. The letter is a masterpiece of clean, honest expression and elegance, more even than Onegin's own letter, written later and too late, declaring his remorse and newfound passion, and offering that she leave her husband and join him, which she will not. In the film, Tatyana's letter is likewise withheld until later in the story, the viewer only getting fragments of cursive script as she writes, lovely though scarred with erasures— "passion," "secret love." The viewer gets the full masterpiece when Onegin pulls it out to read again in his room while in futile pursuit of the now unapproachable wife of the prince his cousin.

> *Dearest Evgeny, I write to you, it is all I can do. And now I know it is in your power to punish my presuming heart. Yet if you have one drop of pity, you'll not abandon me to my unhappy fate. I am in love with you and I must tell you this or my heart, my heart which belongs to you, will surely break. I would never have revealed my shame to you, if just once a week I might see you. Exchange a word or two and then think day and night of one thing alone til our next meeting. But you're unsociable, they say, that the country bores you. Is it true? Does the country bore you? Sometimes I wonder that you ever visited us. Why, I'd never have known you or known this agony and fever. I know that all my life's been leading me to this union with you. I recognised you at first sight and knew with certainty. I said to myself, It's him, he has come. Help me, resolve my doubts. Perhaps all this is nonsense, emptiness, a delusion and quite another fate awaits me. Imagine it, I'm here alone half out of my mind. I dread to read this over, my secret longing. I know that I can trust your honour, though I feel faint from shame and fear,*
> *Tatyana*

Not much can be said after this revelation. It casts too bright a light back to the gazebo where Onegin foolishly rejected the girl's offer. How could he? His sophistication had blinded him, the way culture often blinds even very sensitive critics to true greatness.

Tatyana represents *the beautiful* in the film. Tall, somewhat aloof, elegant in form, with perfect integrity, and as revealed in the letter intelligence. Early in the film, she appears an object of visual allure worthy of Onegin and the viewer's attention. The story of the world-weary man of court coming to the country for respite seems ready for an easy resolution with Tatyana set up to be the thing secretly desired and then obtained in the end. Unless perhaps she is like Olga, made more than she is by Lenski's devotion, but ultimately "easy," as Onegin will cynically go on to prove at the party. That would bring a different kind of tragedy, however, that of a false beauty uncovered, a beauty imposed upon an object from a subjective position. Again, Dietrich von Hildebrand draws a tight distinction,

> *The specific character of being-affected shows us clearly the ontological and qualitative difference between beauty and its "effect" in our soul. It also shows that Beauty is the principium (that which originates), and our being profoundly moved by beauty is the principiatum (that which is originated). It is precisely this touching of the soul by beauty, through the experience of being-affected, that shows us how impossible it is to make beauty a product or a projection of the experience that beauty awakens in us, and that can be awakened only by beauty.*[8]

It is Tatyana's genuine integrity, revealed in the letter and in her final rejection of Onegin's offer to return to him, that her perfections become most apparent. In the end, she cannot assent to his desires because of who and what she is, feelings being secondary. He mistakenly thought his adoration was what made her desirable when all the while her allure was her own.

This context brings us to the climactic scene in which Tatyana turns Onegin away, a scene of exquisite pain that might even move hearts of stone. Fiennes sets it up with a long sequence describing Onegin dressing with the utmost care in preparation to visit his beloved in her lavish home. The camera is behind Onegin as he opens the door into the grand sitting room where Tatyana waits placidly, rendering him a black silhouette against the stark white decor.

The operatic music which accompanies his journey stops as the room is revealed, leaving only his footsteps on the marble to break the silence until she whispers, "Why have you come here?" as a spirit might question a damned soul that wandered into neutral territory. She follows with "You have to leave" and another question, "Why do you pursue me like this?" all delivered in whispers. As he begins to insist on his love, a passion inexplicable even to himself, she questions his motives. Is he in pursuit of a triumph, a brief scandal, is it that she is now noble and worthy of his notice? Her life, despite her wealth, is now empty and hollow, she tells him, and she would exchange it all for the life she once had. Why is he tormenting her further?

The stark setting for the exchange, the lifeless and vast space with so little furniture, presents a visual metaphor for the two of them. Both now live in the sterile world, though hers white and his black. She rises from the divan and moves across the room to a single chair, almost absurdly placed, yet allowing so provocative and definitive a climax. He repeats a version of the question she asked him earlier, "Tell me that you feel nothing." She replies that her husband is asleep upstairs. He then prods her on her heart being healed. "Has it healed? I don't think so." Why does her heart still hurt? She answers emphatically though through tears, "Because you are too late. You are *too* late." At this admission of anguish, he fails again as in the gazebo by pulling the veil to hide his interior life; instead of hearing her in sympathy, he wounds her further with the selfish plea, "Save me. Save me." Her reply, "I cannot save you. I cannot." The music in the background, muted to this point, builds. He insists she tell him that she loves him still, and she confesses, "I love you. I do." Then, however, she declares emphatically, "I am another man's wife. Do you understand, and I have given him my word? And I will be faithful to him." As his face falls on this insistence, she reveals her true spirit, the spirit we have discovered to be as complex and forceful as his own, "And *I will.* You must go. I can never see you again. You can never come back. Please." She leaves him to despair and her iron resolve.

The scene matches the one in the gazebo but in reverse. The wheel has come full circle, and it is indeed untrue. He is cursed and without hope, and she is to suffer as well, though with her integrity still intact. He is damned to hell, she to purgatory. Earlier in the story he had proudly declared that he had no secret longing to be saved from himself, but these last events prove those words false. She spoke truth and is miserable for life. He lied and would not repent of it and has lost his chance at salvation after life. The film concludes with Onegin on a hotel balcony in the cold and then walking through snow down some unnamed street.

The terrible irony of Onegin's fate heightens the effect of the climactic scene in Tatyana's grand home; yet the force of the viewer's anguish stems not from Onegin's damnation but from Tatyana's suffering. The tragedy is really hers, and it affects us because so familiar a purgation. Who has not wept over and again the damning choices made by a loved one? Who has not lived with the painful memories of lost joys caused by those who "curse" themselves, as has Onegin? The moment suggests another incident from Dante, the effect on the poet pilgrim hearing the tragic account of Francesca's doomed love for Paolo,

*As she said this,*
*The other spirit, who stood by her, wept*
*So piteously, I felt my senses reel*
*And faint away with anguish. I was swept*
*By such a swoon as death is, and I fell,*
*As a corpse might fall, to the dead floor of Hell.*

Dante swoons "as a corpse might fall" with the heartbreak of these lovers led astray by the false fancies of romance, their love mistimed, unlawful, and thus damning. Tatyana's sorrow and ours is grounded in Onegin's proud unwillingness to live according to truth until too late, as well as the pitiless movement of cause and effect grinding like the mill blades out of sync.

The poignancy of this conclusion has greater impact than in the Pushkin original because the irony is aligned so closely with deeper truths of spiritual despair, the coldhearted principles of loss we all meet through our lives. By definition, the Byronic hero is subject to the cruel ironies of fate and so worthy of our empathy in the many tales employing his services, and the ending of his misadventures is always tragic and painful, but the pain is not of the degree here, that level of anguish that one carries for years and years. In fact, Pushkin exits his verse novel with a rather light heart,

*Whoever you be, O my reader—*
*friend, foe—I wish with you*
*to part at present as a pal.*
*Farewell. Whatever you in my wake*
*sought in these careless strophes—*
*tumultuous recollections,*
*relief from labours,*
*live pictures or bon mots,*

*or faults of grammar—*
*God grant that you, in this book*
*for recreation, for the daydream,*
*for the heart, for jousts in journals,*
*may find at least a crumb.*
*Upon which, let us part, farewell!*

It is impossible to walk away from Fiennes' *Onegin* with a light heart. The final word is not a pithy anecdote about the danger of pursuing too much knowledge and experience and how following that course can leave one forever outside the sweet comforts of love; rather, it is a proverb about a central truth of common life in a world gone to vanity and subject to the full effects of the loss of Eden, "For in much wisdom is much vexation, and he who increases knowledge increases sorrow" (Proverbs 1: 18). We weep along with Tatyana. Some broken relationships will never be mended. Some loved souls will be forever lost.

# 3

# A RIVER RUNS THROUGH IT

> *We cannot understand. The best is perhaps what we understand least.*
>
> —*C. S. Lewis,* A Grief Observed

When I was thirteen, an old beaten-down calico cat started hanging around the house. Our mother had allergies so no animals inside, but we had been feeding feral cats on the back porch for years, a practice that started when a stray followed me home from the park after an afternoon of baseball in the hot sun; I had been petting it while waiting my turn to bat. The thing was starving and desperate and had apparently decided to throw in for the first child that made serious eye contact, and its act of faith granted it the privilege of becoming the elder in the line of ferals that stalked the porch of our home for years crying for scraps. They remain on the fringes of memory thanks to a single, hazy photograph in an album rarely opened of one such orphan, Fluffy, half-sleep on an old board rotting in the back of the violet patch.

The calico was just like all the rest except leaner and sicker and with a gash on his head. It came up the porch steps wild and uneasy, but after a few weeks coaxing let me touch it and then pet it; once the poor thing purred, the relationship was consummated. It would await my return from school like a desperate lover.

Not long into the affair, though time enough for me to appreciate the distinctness of its cat love, and for it to start looking better, I heard outside the living room window a screech of tires on Ridgeway Street. By the time the crowd gathered, the driver had peeled off. A neighborhood boy on a bicycle held court yelling, "Did you see that? He hit the cat." Then even he rode off leaving just me and the calico, crushed belly but alive for a few minutes staring into death in that distant way of beasts, one eye almost out and tongue lolling. It died as I talked to it. Its bier was a rusty snow shovel from the basement; its coffin a plastic garbage bag. Rolling the limp, bagged thing off the shovel into the can in the alley was the worst moment.

At the time, our mother was lying in a bed in Swedish Covenant Hospital recovering from one of the many ailments that plagued her, and she had instructed me to take the bus that day and visit after the homework was done. Instead, after disposing of the carcass I walked the three miles through the late afternoon gray of Chicago in October. The strategy upon arrival was to hold off telling the story, to be strong and cool perhaps for her sake, but as she turned and smiled and told me to take off my coat and sit down, all I could find to do was fall against the hospital bed into her arms. The tears came in waves.

It feels odd to introduce the subject of loss with just this story long buried in a back room of grief. Many other incidents come to mind now as perhaps more in keeping with academic decorum, but few seem quite so pathetic and sad. And after all, who of us lacks for stories just like this, sorrows rooted in similar memories of lost pets or, Christ have mercy, lost friends and lost parents or children or spouses, and of the uncontrollable tempest that followed such losses, and triggered by the smallest of cues? Though our stories differ in intensity and detail, they share one common trait, helplessness before chance and mortality. Death slaps our face hard when we least expect it. The desire to find appropriate ways to respond to the blow forms the subject of Robert Redford's classic film *A River Runs Through It*.

"Long ago when I was a young man, my father said to me, 'Norman, you like to write stories.' And I said, 'Yes, I do.' Then he said, 'Someday when you're ready you might tell our family story. Only then will you understand what happened and why.'" The words spoken over the hands of the old, fly-fisherman narrator Norman Maclean opens the film and sets the subject of grief as the awful thing to be examined. Loss is tangible like the fishing line and hook the old man baits but elusive like the fish the line is designed to capture. It is a mystery best understood in memory, and that memory demands images and words, forms; yet, all our forms bring us not to an answer, but to question again why the Lord still sleeps in the back of the boat while we suffer the storm. After a fade to black and the introduction of the Elmer Bernstein score, part Celtic and part old West, the title sequence turns us to old photographs of Norman and his brother Paul as boys, and then to the entire family. Tragedy needs victims, even clever and peaceful ones: "In our family, there was no clear line between religion and fly-fishing."

The two boys grow up in Missoula, Montana, at the start of the twentieth century, an era with one leg straddling the frontier past and the other movies and jazz and techno-progress. Norman is older, confident in words like his father, an old Scottish Presbyterian minister who loves to fly-fish and teaches the boys to cast in a perfect four-point rhythm using a metronome. But Paul is the true outdoorsman and genius. He respects his father and brother but describes all his relationships, including those of his trade as newspaper reporter, in the context of his real passion: "You need to take him fishing, Norm," Paul counsels his brother struggling with the destructive behavior of an acquaintance.

We are told that the father to unwind after his sermons would take the boys on a walk along the Big Blackfoot River, their "family river," and speak to them about nature's beauty and the haunting sound of human voices that flow through the Big Blackfoot's waters, the voice of God under the rocks forming the river beds on which those lost souls rest: "But even before that, beneath the rocks are the words of God." He taught the boys to listen, and "if Paul and I listened very carefully all our lives we might hear those words."

This pursuit of the lost through memory underscores not only this film but much of author Norman Maclean's work from *A River Runs Through It* to his posthumous *Young Men and Fire* about thirteen locals who die fighting a Montana forest fire. The theme seems to derive from two sources, Maclean's long career teaching the romantics and Shakespeare at the University of Chicago and the tragic death of his real-life brother Paul in 1938, not in Montana as in the Redford film, but in a back alley in the south side of Chicago with four dollars in his pocket. In the film, Norman asks Paul to come to Chicago with him and his wife Jesse, and Paul refuses, "Oh, I'll never leave Montana, brother." In a way he never did.

It is always a dangerous business trying to interpret a work of art from the fragments we gather of an artist's life. But in the case of Norman Maclean, a significant aspect of his thinking clearly aligned with the gentle romanticism he taught, nature as deeply interfused with the presence of its creator. Another and darker aspect questioned the loving personal God his father preached—the tragedy of his brother and the related effects of his brother's life on his parents. Perhaps this joined the Shakespearean influence, as his stories repeat questions found in the tragedies. Why should Cordelia die at the end of Lear? The daughter and father have reconciled in that most poignant scene, "Do not laugh at me;/ For as I am a man, I think this lady/ To be my child Cordelia." Still she dies unfairly and unjustly, and Lear must carry her corpse across the stage wondering aloud why she lacks the breath that beasts enjoy, "Why should a dog, a horse, a rat, have life, And thou no breath at all?" Shakespeare had lost his own son Hamnet at age eleven a decade before, and evidence suggests he was likely present when the Jesuit poet saint, Robert Southwell, was hung, drawn, and quartered.[9]

In *Young Men and Fire*, MacLean analyzed the Mann Gulch Fire northeast of Helena, Montana, a fire that claimed the lives of thirteen parachuting firefighters in 1949 when the winds suddenly shifted and brought the blaze into and around the men.

> *Although the Mann Gulch fire occurred early in the history of the Smokejumpers, it is still their special tragedy, the one in which their crew suffered almost a total loss and the only one in which their loss came from the fire itself.*[10]

The entire premise of that book is an attempt to explain the seemingly inexplicable, to find rational causality when ordinary reason seems to fail. And so, in *A River Runs Through It*, Maclean examines the loss of his younger brother Paul and the exquisite grief that would hover over his parents' and his faith afterward. As Job expressed it, "Wherefore is light given to him that is in misery, and life unto the bitter in soul?"

*A River Runs Through It* plays that question *why* in several scenes but principally as a hollow echo against the harmonious goodness of God evidenced in the nature that interfuses the setting of the film. Robert Redford frames the question with sweeping images of the Big Blackfoot River and the hills of Montana and the fresh and handsome faces of Brad Pitt and Craig Sheffer, the young actors who play Paul and Norman.

The climax occurs in tragic counterpoint. First comes a long, beautifully shot sequence of Paul demonstrating his shadow-casting technique and catching a prize trout, his line floating lightly across the water in slow-motion with the score singing behind those lovely motions. He nearly drowns in the effort, going through rapids with his arm along raised above the water holding the line before gracefully emerging like one newly baptized. Norman and his father watch in tense admiration, and then celebrate as Paul displays the catch. Norman provides voiceover commentary, "At that moment I knew, surely and clearly, that I was witnessing perfection." They take photos, and the voiceover continues, "My brother stood before us not on the bank of the Big Blackfoot River, but suspended above the earth, free from all its laws, like a work of art. And I knew just as surely and just as clearly that life is not a work of art and that the moment could not last." Art cannot last in a fallen world. People cannot live free from cause and effect as Paul has tried to do. Romanticism always seems to lead from the rolling, pastoral hills of Wordsworth to the devil ship of Coleridge. The image of the river waters glistening in the dusk, music softly accompanying the reverie, the image of the triumphant Paul so handsome in close-up—this all cuts directly to the doors of the police station in the silence of the morning. "And so, when the police sergeant awakened me one morning just before Jessie and I left for Chicago, I rose and asked no questions." Paul had been beaten to death with the butt of a revolver, evidently by thugs sent to collect his gambling debts.

The scene had been foreshadowed earlier in the movie with three sequences played one against the other. Paul and Norman go out with their dates, Jesse with Norman and Paul bringing an Indian girl with a bad reputation, Mabel. They dance, and Paul shows his innate charm and indifference to society, easing Mabel through a provocative number and then swinging her through the Muskrat Ramble. That sequence leads to the counterpoint, Jesse reading a beautiful love letter in which Norman makes good an allusion from Wordsworth to suggest that she makes the land even more beautiful for him, "…my mind is filled with song. I find I am humming softly, not to the music, but something else. Someplace else. A place remembered. A field of grass where no one seemed to have been, except the deer, and the memory is strengthened by the feeling of you dancing in my awkward arms." The letter is accompanied by images of the scenery around the Big Blackfoot in the morning. That scene then cuts back as abruptly to one foreshadowing the scene describing Paul's death. Though here, it is the house that is silent. Norman answers the phone and is sent by a caller to the same police station. Paul had gotten into a fight over a comment against his Indian girlfriend. The desk sergeant removes his glasses to confront Norman, "We're picking your brother up too much lately. Besides, he's behind in the big stud poker game at Lolo. It's not healthy to get behind at Lolo." As Norman descends to Paul's cell, the sounds are exaggerated and hollow. Footsteps, keys in a lock, a door creaking open, a drunk singing an old song, the cell opening; then Paul, blood on his cuff, points unsteadily toward Mabel asleep on the concrete. Paul motions Norman to drag her out, the camera watching from metaphoric floor level.

Redford's film continually teases the viewer with depictions of that gentler romanticism before shifting hard to the probing questions it means to ask—what is the dark force driving so many whom we love toward the precipice of self-destruction; just what is that dark principle that will not allow peace to continue in this life? Nature speaks of her grace and beauty, and the atheist cannot remain long at the fishing hole on a crisp, bright morning when a fisherman expects to see "a rainbow rise." Yet, abruptly the umbilical cord is sheared, and our pastoral dreams shift hard into blackness and silence.

The narrator of the film—Redford chose the role for himself—speaks for Norman, whose Presbyterian father "believed that man, by nature, was a damned mess, and that only by picking up God's rhythms" are we able to regain power and beauty. To Norman's father, all good things, trout as well as eternal salvation, come as result of labor leading to grace. It is a philosophy Thomas Aquinas would have approved. "And grace comes by art, and art does not come easy." These words accompany images of the father carefully putting on his fishing glove to demonstrate the proper system of casting. Norman and Paul learned to cast by that metronome and so learned the art of fishing as craft not recreation. All good things come that way, careful conception and execution. It is the only way forward in a fallen world overgrown and spottily managed, so affirms the old preacher. Paul tries this as a youth casting a fly in four-point rhythm over the waters, but not through the course of his life. He refuses to stay with the metronome, too strongly tempted by the sweet songs of the magic river and too constitutionally stubborn to adhere to a manmade rule. Paul will become a "fine fisherman," in his father's words, and "beautiful," but not according to the metronome philosophy. He becomes beautiful by pure natural improvisation, indomitably free from hard laws, and so doomed in this world. Early in the film we watch Paul sit before a bowl of uneaten oatmeal for hours until his father gives up the attempt to mold that will.

Norman tells the story seemingly in the hope that a salvific ending will come as result of the telling, having spent years mastering his specific language of grief; but in the end he is still searching for the right words. And just so, we seek in our endeavors, be they as humble as those of the poor fisherman, a way to see how the grace of God will redeem our losses. We place our hopes in heaven from what we have heard of it in our lessons. And we had those lessons reinforced in those revealing glimpses from nature, what William Wordsworth, old mentor to the professor Maclean, called "spots of time" when past and present meet in a harmony not of human origin. The damned mess of humanity troubles, even dominates, so often; and yet the other voice keeps teasing us along toward the belief that yes, the pain will be overcome, the struggle will lead somewhere. We see the beauty of the rapids and wonder why they would ever swallow us alive?

Recently in my own exercise of language learning, I discovered my students were moved through reading Charles Lamb's famous poem "The Old Familiar Faces,"

> *How some they have died, and some they have left me,*
> *And some are taken from me; all are departed—*
> *All, all are gone, the old familiar faces.*

Lamb found his words through the tragedy of his own family, his troubled sister Mary having killed their mother with a kitchen knife during a fit of dementia. Lamb would care for his sister the rest of her life, even co-authoring with her a retelling of Shakespeare plays for children. Such forgiving love is what moved my students, an imagined scene coalesced in the mind's eye of an old kitchen floor with Lamb and sister and dying mother covered in blood and wailing together; then another scene much later with Lamb tenderly asking his sister Mary how she is feeling today after catching a distant look in her eye. Perhaps she had just turned toward her kitchen window which framed a cluster of children brawling outside and wondered how these children would find a path forward, how they would respond to the old familiar faces which would later haunt them.

Forms we discover in the mist of memory colored through imagination, old loves, the old familiar faces of our family—these we place in a line as the older Norman does. Few films evoke the process as effectively. Paul is beautiful on the river and in spots of his normal life, as in the golden hour leaning up over the windshield of his car telling his beloved brother Norman that he is not funny, which really means he loves him and recognizes his love for Jesse, his girl. Paul is so alive and mostly so very good.

The character of Jesse Burns mirrors Norman when it comes to grief. Her brother Neal, a fool and vain boaster addicted to cheap alcohol and women, comes to visit, and she cannot guide him enough for change. When he sneaks away from a family get-together, Jesse urges Norman to follow, hoping Norman can save Neal and bring him back to the family. He cannot, nor will he be able to stop the inevitable when Paul will likewise slip away from a family dinner, not to visit a drinking hole as Neal does, but Lolo Hot Springs where he is losing consistently at the big stud poker game. He shouldn't be drinking so much; they don't drink too much at the big poker game at Lolo. Who has not seen the pain on some poor parent's face when the wandering child wanders, when no human love seems able to stop this flight, or explain why? We form reasonable arguments that convince only those already convinced to stir up energy to fight the indomitable will that always eludes our pleas.

Alcoholism runs in my family. I carry only a few memories of the days before several close relatives were lost in it, of lovely faces and long legs and perpetual cheerfulness that turned large and indolent. Those images remain small parts of a dreary montage of quarrels and glassy eyes gazing dreamily toward the ceiling and incoherent stories of who was to blame and why, and then pathetic attempts at suicide and the ensuing shame and half reconciliations. We don't have the right key to the doors. "Why is it that people who need the most help won't take it?" Jesse asks Norman after Neal boards the train to return to nowhere. "I don't know, Jess," Norman replies. It is the author's response, too, the older Norman looking back and grieving his beautiful brother Paul. That tragic moment is relieved by Norman's revelation that the University of Chicago has invited him to pursue a degree and teach literature. "The truth is, I'm not sure I want to leave," he admits to

Jesse. Montana will always be here, she says. "Not Montana… I'm not sure I want to leave you." It's a proposal, hope out of despair, and she embraces him, a transcendent moment in the film that tugs on us to believe more is possible than the mortal storm pulling us down. Here is Jesse as the girl with the ponytail and Norman as the awkward boy from town and all of heaven looking down upon the naïve lovers as happened in the beginning when Adam named Eve the mother of the living, mother of all our broken loves.

The film has several such moments. When Norman is back home from Dartmouth, his father calls him into the study to ask about his sense of vocation. It's an awkward conversation, yet familiar, the colliding of youthful freedom with the adult world of responsibility. Norman's manner expresses a certain pity for his father stuck in an old man's body and mind as he is, but he tries his best to answer as he should. There is deep love even in the awkward exchange. Then in a later scene, Norman walks in on his father quoting Wordsworth's "Ode: Intimations of Immortality" in the same study, and the two share a genuine moment of understanding,

*Though nothing can bring back the hour*
*Of splendour in the grass, of glory in the flower;*
*We will grieve not, rather find*
*Strength in what remains behind;*
*In the primal sympathy*
*Which having been must ever be;*
*In the soothing thoughts that spring*
*Out of human suffering;*
*In the faith that looks through death,*
*In years that bring the philosophic mind.*

Sons don't know their fathers well, and we fathers don't often know or understand our sons, but in spots of time we can connect, and through memory we can pull such moments together to form a coherent past that provides us the foundation of words to describe something, the way experience cannot. Benevolent providence intrudes upon chance in the form of constructed memory to reassure us that all may still be well. The relationship between Norman and his father feels slightly distant throughout the novel and film, but in these few moments they are united in spirit, as when Norman will sit in a pew and listen to his father eulogize Paul. Norman's eyes reveal a new sympathy through their shared grief.

Nature pure as the sun on the Big Blackfoot in so many of the fishing scenes pulls us as well toward these more hopeful truths. When Paul catches that prize trout in the rapids of the river, his pole held high in one end above the turbulent waters, he shows himself a work of art and part of that secret rhythm that invites grace. Norman and their father watch in admiration, and Norman memorializes Paul, "At that moment I knew surely and clearly that I was witnessing perfection." Then after a photo, "My brother stood before us not on the Big Blackfoot but suspended above the earth, free from all its laws, like a work of art." The moment could not and does not last as the scene dissolves into the rolling river which turns to Norman arriving at the police station at night to receive the tragic news he will need share with his stunned parents. Yet the image still lingers in the mind as truer than the bloody event off screen. Memory constructed in a coherence that allows for words is beautiful, heavenly.

Paul is not free from nature's law, nor is Norman, nor are we watching. Nature cradles us in her rigid mesh of consequence and rocks us to a final sleep in patterns we do not understand, whether formed from the infamy of drunkenness and unchecked vice or in a quiet life of sanctity, and always with dreams of those we have lost. Paul's innocent world on the river was his attempt to push beyond the law of life to a different life with no dark consequence, toward hope more permanent than our calamitous mortality allows. His story arc offers an argument against natural consequence, even though Norman and his parents can only see it as an argument against the God who grants such dangerous freedom, the world's governor who seems to promise relief only once all the hands are played out. All the stories clustered together affirm at least the possibility of triumph beyond the tragedies.

The film unfolds these realities like a classic argument. Youthful innocence countered by the brawling physicality that defined manhood in Montana, care of the land and nature versus reckless adventurousness, a drink shared amongst friends versus drinks under the table in flasks, quiet domesticity versus red-dressed and heedless sexuality. When Jesse reads that letter from Norman echoing Wordsworth's blessing on his own sister, we feel an exquisite pain. The ruined Tintern Abbey is lost to sight but resurrected more beautiful through memory, the poet's blended with those of his Dorothy.

> *Nor wilt thou then forget,*
> *That after many wanderings, many years*
> *Of absence, these steep woods and lofty cliffs,*
> *And this green pastoral landscape, were to me*
> *More dear, both for themselves and for thy sake!*

In the letter Norman calls to mind a pristine field with the burst of insects flying out to greet the morning and provide for all the living, and that image is made stronger by that of Jesse dancing in his "awkward arms." When the scene cuts from his romantic letter to the phone ringing with the police calling for Paul to be taken home from jail, we fear Paul in the underworld is lost forever. But then he goes off to play cards again only to appear for a few days longer his old self ready to go fishing with his brother. Redford in Shakespearian style places Paul's death, like Cordelia's, off stage. We don't witness it happen, just its aftermath, and so it is less real than our memories of him in his glowing vitality and artistic triumph. This can't be all, can it? There must be more than just this.

So it is in life that our holidays and birthdays get muddied by quarrels and drunkenness and old resentments. And we go from bliss to misery and hardly know how one turned to the other or what can reverse the momentum. The ones we love choose a different bed for the night or a different home, and we find ourselves trapped in a game of destruction, knowing what needs to be said and done but incapable of settling our will in the correct direction. We have no certain understanding why the destructive impulses come as they do and very little power to control them. So, we give in and blame heaven for the freedom that enables us to both love and murder. Later in quiet reflection the parts come back, and the ones that carry the most strength and linger the longest are of forgiveness and mercy and life. It didn't really occur, did it? All the losses will be restored, and sorrows ended, won't they?

We cry when memory or art brings us back to the ash pile of our ruined dreams. We don't grieve the onset of loneliness so much as we do the inadequacy of our own words and deeds to redeem the moment, our inability to take it all in and see through. And in those griefs, we yearn for the ear of the intention behind it all, the source of the art our lives never quite realized. The river runs through our stories and the words underneath haunt each of us. Norman's father offers one way forward in the sermon fragment hovering over the film's conclusion, "It is true we can seldom help those closest to us. Either we don't know what part of ourselves to give or more often than not, the part we have to give is not wanted. And so it is those we live with and should know who elude us, but we can still love them. We can love completely without complete understanding." Those words dissolve into a recollection of the two brothers fishing in the half light and then of the old Norman narrating that those he loved and did not understand are gone, but he still reaches out to them. "Eventually all things merge into one and a river runs through it." It is a biblical allusion for all who come from the earth and dissolve back into it. The river carries the lives of our people loved and lost who now play in and out of memory and the mind of God.

The film concludes with the older Norman Maclean's confession, "I am haunted by waters," a good confession of guilt and inadequacy and dependence. We listen and agree that we all grieve those we so imperfectly love. Alongside our hearts console us we were always meant for something else, not this, something better; life moves from a single source and is collected in a final end, but for a purpose that we can only feel deep in our throat and in our bones, a wordless revelation promising a day of Jubilee.

> *Thou hearest every prayer offered to thee believingly with a penitent and sincere heart. For thou in withholding grantest, healest in inflicting the wound, yea, turnest all to good for as many as truly seek thee through Christ, the Mediator!*

In 1831 the poet Samuel Taylor Coleridge, troubled by guilt over lost opportunities stirred in the cup of his gnawing laudanum addiction only partially controlled, prayed, "O in thy mercy vouchsafe me yet in this my decay of life an interval of ease and strength." Coleridge was Wordsworth's dear friend until his insecurity and weakness caused a breach in the relationship for over a decade. He had many long evenings to lament his folly, the end of a fellowship time only allows on rare occasions. It was a strained prayer, but sincere and likely heard, a prayer that looked through the facts of the tragedy to a hope for consolation and restoration.

*A River Runs Through It* has few faults and one great virtue: it tells us the truth about hope. What are we without the hope of heaven, without some possibility of a perfect mercy bathing our wounds and returning us to play in the grass and fish in the Big Blackfoot once again? We are less than the beasts without such. All losses must be restored and sorrows need to end or to what purpose is the crisp air in the morning with the smell of grass and forest and the sound of the birds just beginning to sing? To what purpose?

# 4

# BABETTE'S FEAST

> *To whom hath the root of wisdom been revealed, and who hath known her wise counsels? To whom hath the discipline of wisdom been revealed and made manifest? and who hath understood the multiplicity of her steps?*
>
> —Ecclesiasticus

God meant this evil for good. Those are the words of Israel's son Joseph, hated by his brothers, rejected then sold into slavery, falsely imprisoned, forgotten. When he unexpectedly shows up alive after his ascent to Pharaoh's right hand, his brothers are convinced he will have them killed for their crimes, but Joseph sees a different providence. God tore him from the living as He would his own Son so that many could be saved. Joseph's trail of misery led inextricably to his position of power, and exactly that hard journey transformed him into a man capable of exercising power correctly.

At times we all experience such a mysterious providence and feel a similar tremor of awe, though few of us have such grand ambitions as Joseph inadvertently achieved. We pray and hope, and then one day the threads come together in some unexpected fashion. It is not a matter of better choices leading to better ends either; matters just seem to arrange for once in our favor. And only God could design the pattern they form, we come to believe.

A film that moves along this line is Gabriel Axel's *Babette's Feast* (1987). *Babette's Feast* received the Academy Award for Best Foreign-Language Film in 1988 and then the BAFTA for best non-English language film in 1989. Its accolades came from all quarters, secular and religious, and touched on all its elements from storytelling to characterization to visual aesthetics. Its internal energy and power have proven infectious to the degree where three decades later people will still reference it anecdotally to make a point about food, fellowship, or love—*this reminds me of that scene in Babette's Feast where the sectarians agree to say nothing about the food. Remember that?*

Curious yet fitting is how accidental this masterpiece seems upon examination. The material that Axel was presented and eventually realized in the film came from an Isak Dinesen short story found in her 1953 collection *Anecdotes of Destiny*. Dinesen, Karen Blixen, had come back broke from an extravagant vacation with friends in Venice in 1949. To catch up she decided to try publishing in the lucrative American market, and a friend, the anthropologist Geoffrey Gorer, made a bet with her that she could not make it into the popular *Saturday Evening Post*. Dinesen took him up and asked what kind of material the American public most liked to read. Gorer told her, "Write about food. Americans are obsessed with food." So, she wrote "Babette's Feast," which *The Post*... rejected.[11] Fortunately for the world, *Ladies' Home Journal* published it in 1950.

Neither Dinesen nor Axel seemed to have set out with the intention of composing a polemic on divine providence. Dinesen came from Unitarian stock and maintained a long-standing interest in myth, philosophy, and psychology, not Christian pastoral theology. Axel was most known for directing and performing in Danish comedies in the 50s and 60s, some of questionable content. It is equally questionable that either would have anticipated the effects the film would have, although signs suggest that others did see it, if only based on the brilliant cast of European film luminaries that Axel was able to lure to the project.

Axel adapted the Dinesen tale with only a few modifications which he would claim rendered the film more faithful to its original. The location was changed from Norway to the Jutland coast in the director's native Denmark. This allowed him to render the "grey, yellow, pink and other colors" of Dinesen's description of locale to the steel grey and white of that region, shades he believed more reflective of the austerity of the sectarians who reside there in the tale. The move also allowed a greater visual contrast between the local inhabitants and the outsider Babette who comes as a refugee from a more richly-textured Paris to live in seclusion after the murder of her husband and son by the Paris Commune. Also altered are the characterizations of the two principals, Babette and General Lorens Löwenhielm whose two visits to the village bookend the story's action. Löwenhielm comes across as far more a romantic in the film than on paper, a shift in character that renders his reflections at and after the banquet especially affecting. Babette, played by the graceful Stéphane Audran, carries more nuance and interiority than the stoical figure in the original story. Dinesen tells the reader that Babette was a Communard who supplied arms to her husband and son during the 1871 Paris uprising. That type hardly describes the actress, and Axel wisely omits the political detail, leaving her simply a martyr to a vague, alien cause, and a widow.

The plot follows Babette, the refugee French chef, but its pivot is the fate of two Danish sisters, Martine and Filippa, the repressed yet dutiful daughters of a strict and controlling pietist widower who has founded and maintained the small sect of true believers in the little Jutland village bordering the vast North Sea. The sisters are introduced in a voiceover and followed from young womanhood to old age when Babette enters the village and then serves them fourteen years until the climactic events. Both sisters are courted once seriously by outsiders, Martine by Löwenhielm and Filippa by Achille Papin, a star of the Parisienne stage. However, their pietist father, "well-respected, and perhaps also a little feared," coerces the daughters to remain true to the cause by serving the community unmarried as his right and left hands. His selfishness is reinforced by the asceticism he has taught all the members of his sect—the glories of heaven so far outweigh the temporal pleasures of earthly life that it is best to give those pleasures up all together.

The failed love affairs drive the sorrows in the film. When Martine is courted by the young Löwenhielm, he is introduced as a somewhat dissolute officer of the hussars who has been sent by his commanding officer for a three-month stay to mend his ways under the watchful eye of his devout aunt in the Jutland. As the aunt is part of the minister's little flock, Löwenhielm is granted means to spend time with the beautiful Martine whom he spots when out riding one lonely morning. After a valiant effort to develop a relationship with her, he eventually grows disillusioned with the growing coldness of the minister and its unnatural result, the distancing of the heart of his beloved. He tells Martine he will leave and never return; then once back in his brigade, he declares his intention to put such vaporous dreams behind him and cut a brilliant figure in the world, in effect offering a challenge to heaven and the lofty promises of religion. Filippa is courted sometime later by Papin, who has grown weary of the Parisienne public life of a singer and been encouraged to visit the Jutland by a friend who tells him no place will provide more solitude. When he arrives, he is instead overwhelmed with a sense of his own insignificance, broken only when he hears like a siren in the distance the beautiful voice of Filippa singing a hymn with the small flock gathered at the minister's church. Quickly determining that she is a great diva hidden away from the world, he asks the minister if he can provide her voice lessons. The lessons progress too well, however, a sequence culminating with the two singing a love duet from Mozart leading the minister to apply his paternal prerogative again, and Filippa breaks it off. Papin reads her letter brokenhearted and leaves the village as had Löwenhielm to return to the world crushed in spirit.

The story resumes many years later as the spinster sisters struggle to hold the congregation together after the minister's death. The pettiness of the minister's venture into pietism has filtered down through the now elderly and cantankerous band of true believers. Salvation comes when on a stormy night a boat brings Babette to the village with a letter of introduction from Papin to Filippa requesting that the widow be given refuge, adding in ironic brevity that "Babette can cook." So, Babette begins her service to the sisters and flock, blessing them all with far better gruel and the sisters with more space to do their work thanks to her resource and ingenuity in domestic management.

The fourteen years pass uneventfully until Babette receives a letter indicating that a French lottery ticket she has renewed each year through a friend has won her 10,000 francs. At this she requests of the sisters the privilege of making the celebratory dinner for the upcoming centennial of the minister's birth. Unaware of what this implies, the sisters agree. The meal becomes an elaborate affair of wines and European delicacies, and a surprise visitor to the event, the now General Löwenhielm, the only one at table who realizes just how extraordinary a gift Babette has given. The other sectarians have vowed to not speak of the pleasures of the meal which they take as a temptation coming from the devil through their beloved but still papist cook. Nonetheless, the food wins over the group in eucharistic fashion, leading them to resolve old quarrels, and leading Löwenhielm to reaffirm his love for Martine, not in body but in his soul which is all that he claims now matters, for he has come to realize that through God's mercy "all things are possible."

In the conclusion, Martine and Filippa thank their surprising cook assuming she will soon be leaving with the remains of her winnings, but Babette reveals that she spent the entire 10,000 francs on the feast. She was the head chef at the Café Anglais in Paris and recognized as *the* great culinary artist of the day. The celebratory meal was to bless them, she says, but also for herself, as artists long for the opportunity to do their best. Filippa, who understands this kind of sacrifice in her own way, embraces Babette and offers a better perspective, that in heaven she will delight the angels with her gift, echoing words spoken to her by Papin, that her voice lost to the world will one day delight the angels.

In the Dinesen original, Babette's sacrifice is principally the triumph of art over rationalism. Art reveals the beauty and purpose of human experience from joy to sorrow, love gained to forever lost. It allows "righteousness and bliss" and "mercy and truth" to kiss as the General quotes from the Psalms in his toast at the table. Babette's meal bridges the chasm between the paucity of the stiff sectarians and the excesses of court represented by the General and Papin.

The film offers other dimensions of meaning and a deeper emotional effect. The comedy of the reconciliation is played in full in the sequence describing the table farce where the humble guests eat sumptuous food and sip the finest of wines but refuse to verbalize the delights of the flesh their eyes behold and palates savor. An especially tender scene follows this one that enjoys strong support from the film's melancholy and memorable score. In the hall Martine searches the face of her long-lost beloved now General with secret joy sparkling through her moist eyes, after which Löwenhielm departs her, stepping onto his carriage with chivalrous dignity, the knight commissioned to carry their love in a sacred pouch through the remainder of his long, weary days. In a similar way, the film closes the loop tighter involving Philippa and Papin whose disillusionment is vicariously redeemed by the success of Babette's communal feast: his earlier letter of introduction had been read by Martine with interspersed images of the old and heavy singer in his lonely, world-weary dotage; the meal brings their lost love to resolution through the expressions of surprised satisfaction on her face as she looks around the table and then later as she leads the group in an old hymn. The Axel film also better dissolves the class distinctions implicit in the story—all are made one, Babette and the General and

Papin and the sisters, as well as the common villagers and servants at table whose look and mannerisms put on display their simplicity and humanity.

Babette's meal bridges human choice and divine mystery. Both the young Löwenhielm and Papin interpret the minister's rejection of their overtures of love as a signal that human choice can never achieve harmony with divine will or fate. Löwenhielm declares life "hard and cruel." Papin has his sense of insignificance at the vast solitude of the Jutland coast reinforced when upon receiving the minister's letter of dismissal, he resignedly wishes goodbye to all his hopes. Both desperate conclusions are overturned in the end. Babette's feast unites heaven and earth, perfect beauty and love, the depths of human longing and the patience of saints. All the vanities of the world evaporate at that table of eucharistic fellowship to be replaced by tokens of divine promise. Löwenhielm's toast offers the benediction:

> *We have all of us been told that grace is to be found in the universe. But in our human foolishness and shortsightedness we imagine divine grace to be finite. For this reason we tremble. We tremble before making our choice in life, and after making it again tremble in fear of having chosen wrong. But the moment comes when our eyes are opened, and we realize that grace is infinite. Grace, my friends, demands nothing from us but that we shall await it with confidence and acknowledge it in gratitude. Grace, brothers, makes no conditions and singles out none of us in particular; grace takes us all to its bosom and proclaims general amnesty.*

The art of Babette has reconciled the incongruities of choice and loss for the remnant community. The poor bereft lovers find blessing in what they have given up and in what they have chosen, the camera bringing this home poignantly through closeups of the two sisters enraptured with the unexpected pleasures of eating gourmet food and drinking rare wine in the soft, amber glow of their usually dreary dining room, Martine and the General bathed in the glow and exchanging admiring glances. The elderly sectarians find opportunity to speak nostalgically of their former days with the minister and to reconcile their grudges. In Dinesen's original this new harmony is muted by placing much more emphasis on Babette who impassively declares that she willingly gave her family to the cause of the Communards and that she is a "great artist." Her bold posturing is absent in the film, replaced by words and glances reflective and deeply felt. While Dinesen's version is laced with the irony of her mentors of form, Maupassant and Chekhov, Axel's is a more traditional, redemptive tale.

This difference between original story and film rendition is in part a byproduct of the unique iconography of cinematic language, the psychological effects that visual images and sounds create as opposed to mere words entering the imagination of a reader. In the film, we see the sisters suffer and rejoice directly through the camera lens and through Babette's eyes; we watch Babette's hands prepare the food and hear her sighs from the intent labor, and we watch her lips touch the wine glass and drink, and so we taste the wine through her. The latter experience is enhanced because these are the eyes and hands and lips of Stéphane Audran, one of Europe's more graceful film beauties. She the beloved film diva dominates every composition she enters with her warm yet dignified bearing, and her presence before us adds a richness to the way we participate in the story, new readings beyond what appeared on the original magazine pages. Instead of the cool irony of Dinesen's narrator, the camera offers sympathy bathed in Babette's warmth and love. She places a softening gauze over the whole affair.

Likewise, the kitchen where Babette works and the room where the folks dine as well as the outside sitting room where they later sing and reminisce are soaked in the comforting light of stove and candle, the physical realities of that period of time experienced in an immediate way. The entirety of the gray world of the minister's house is transformed in the final sequence to domestic peace and nostalgic dreaminess. The brown and golden hues cast the participants in the kindest of ways.

The loving tone of the conclusion has been foreshadowed from the scene documenting Babette's first entrance to the minister's home, a place the viewer has come to know as pinched and doomed. Prior to Babette's arrival, table arrangements appeared rigid and symmetrical, the backgrounds muted in a cloudy, rectangular blandness. Once Babette appears with the rain on her hair and cloak and the desperation of loss played across her face, the spaces are transformed, the room where the sisters receive their new cook now a refuge of mutual sympathy for all three suffering women, each softened by the warm coloring of a table lamp. The reading of Papin's letter in this intimate setting heightens the effect, recalling for the women and film viewers the cruel judgments that have led to this unlikely fellowship. The viewer begins to feel this thus far stiff and sad film may still end well.

Two earlier scenes set up the transformation, each signaling the loss the younger women experienced from the tyranny of their father. In the first, Martine looks down the path that Löwenhielm follows in his departure, her eyes full of wet confusion and despair; Filippa will later ask her sister one dark evening if she remembers the young soldier who called upon her, causing Martine to turn quietly her bed and utter one word, "yes." Likewise, after Papin's departure, the two women sit quietly reading, the minister behind them feigning attention only to his book. A crosscut shows Papin's boat departing, tossed by the unsympathetic waves of the sea. Can this be all? The answer comes shortly after when Babette will arrive on those same waves. No, heaven sees and has remembered. In both scenes the beautiful face of the women yanked away from the joys of romantic love is registered by a kindly camera, setting a hope that love may still return for them, which it does.

The transitional device used to bring the older stories fourteen years forward to the finale at the feast is an oft-depicted, still composition. Babette sits alone with rolling brown hills behind her, the setting sun coloring the sky; she is positioned to the right in the frame while looking offscreen left. After this fixed shot in the film, she rises gracefully, a small basket in her hands, and crosses the frame left, sanctifying the space as it were, beauty and grace and patience on the move to redeem the conflicts troubling the land. The healthy physicality of Babette suggests change is coming, an answer to the usual angularity of the two old spinsters. Her ease of manner suggests that her own exile was willed, unlike that of Martine and Filippa. She remains the master of her own space and time. The contrast had been evident in earlier compositions around the meal and meeting table. The sisters always sit together, symmetrical and stiff, framed within the windows behind them, confined by the room's narrow walls. Babette, on the other hand, moves easily wherever she is. In the climactic kitchen scenes where she reigns the queen of culinary art, she plies her skill quickly and confidently, and is admired for it by the servants observing, the boy who helps serve the table and the General's carriage driver who alone seems to appreciate fully the miracle taking place. Babette is the antithesis of the unbudging, domineering minister father, who at this point in the story retains his hawkish presence only in the comic form of a portrait prominently displayed on a wall. Babette breaks the household symmetries when she passes, and so breaks the spell. The congregants relax and breathe under her reign.

Perceptions are dominant in the film, as visually suggested by the many compositions involving windows. Babette's initial duties at the house include throwing water upon and wiping the panes of the window glass, as if making it possible for the sisters to look out at the world as it is. When inside, the sisters consistently look away from the windows as if under the Lady of Shalott's curse, damsels imprisoned in a tower. In an earlier sequence Martine shows Babette how to make the local ale bread, a dreary gruel, after which Babette sits alone in her room looking out at the sea and her lost comfortable life. The effect is sad, but still the camera declares that her eyes are turned toward life not death; a villager walking a dog nearby appears within her view. In a subsequent scene the sisters sit at table attempting unsuccessfully to reconcile quarreling members of the flock, and again the grey windows frame them. As if in response, a crosscut displays a glorious sunset shimmering across the sky, presage of the awaiting grace that will eventually bring the entire community together again through the sacramental means of the feast. Then follows a montage—a ringing church bell, Babette quietly at her table looking out, rain falling against the panes which conspicuously suggest a cross—Babette wears one throughout. This shifts back to another short scene with sectarians quarreling at table, Martine and Filippa impotent to help. Babette enters with tea and restores order.

Grace has travelled across the lonely sea despite its expanse and merciless waves, walking over the waters as it were to visit the poor souls locked in the prison of this well-meaning but misguided sect. At the feast, congregants will remind each other of a time when the minister himself seemed to walk on water to offer the means of salvation to community members. God is both infinite and kind. One needs only wait and receive, as the General pronounces in his toast. We fear the curse, but the curse is made the instrument of blessing by divine mercy acting through providence. Babette's arrival and sacramental gift becomes our own. Perhaps a better world existed for all of us once before, we wonder, before the minister and his ilk forced it into a bottle.

We are urged to contemplate the mysterious sea in several ways. Papin and Babette both travel the sea, while the sectarians seem imprisoned by it. Löwenhielm reflects upon the mystery in his toast: "Our choice is of no importance. We come to realize that mercy is infinite. We need only await it with confidence and receive it with gratitude." Infinite mercy for the sisters arrived by boat with Papin and Babette the angelic messengers. Seemingly grim circumstance may have led all these poor souls to choose contrary to what they most desired; yet, Babette's feast restores all those losses.

The sea carries the mystery which all the characters pine for and come to understand, albeit partially, only at the end. Papin experiences a melancholy when he arrives in the Jutland and is confronted by "silence and the sound of the waves." But then his wistful mood is broken by the beautiful sound of Filippa singing in the town church. There is love in her song. He follows Filippa's angelic voice into that small church, crosses himself, and sits admiringly in the back, a smile lighting his face as he beholds Filippa beside her sister in a front pew. But what is Filippa singing? "God is God even if all life were ended." Papin gives God thanks for leading him to a diva, but he misses the cue of the hymn itself. Grace comes through suffering and loss, not through the stage and worldly fame. The camera turns momentarily to the crucifix in front where a smiling, benevolent Christ hangs in repose, striking in its difference from most depictions, but so fitting here. The entire message of the film may very well be captured in that one icon. Only through suffering comes the promise of permanent joy.

This truth finds fullest articulation in the meal sequence, of course, but it is set up by an earlier scene with the old General confronting his younger self in a mirror as he dresses to leave. "Vanity, vanity, all is vanity," he challenges his younger self, seated in silence, arms folded. The older man thus questions through the glass of time his youthful decision to turn from what his disappointment termed foolishness and cut a figure in the world instead—to be happy. "Tonight, we shall settle our score," the old General declares. The score is less one with himself, more with the inscrutable design of things and the seeming capriciousness of chance, and the divine mind behind both. This scene cuts to the sisters praying God's will be done and Babette preparing her signature *Cailles en sarcophagi*, the answer foretold.

The kitchen details that describe the preparations for the meal suggest the true heaven where the stew of events is stirred and then dished out for poor mortals. Unlike the grey austerity of the house and the rest of the village under the minister's spell, the kitchen displays a variety of color and texture, a magical place with magical power. Later when the meal is over, the sectarians move outside to hold hands around a well and celebrate in song how close the stars look, how immediate and gentle heaven now seems.

The film's final revelation is of Babette's former position as head chef at the Café Anglais in Paris and the enormity of the cost she has incurred to bring the sisters and sectarians and General and Papin together. But there is no arrogance in her manner. Babette speaks her words reflectively, as though once more tracing the logic of her choices. She proclaims the triumph of art but in a personal, not universal, sense; that is, the triumph of her special art, her culinary gift. Filippa responds with the broader statement of principle. Art can reconcile in moments, but grace is the ultimate healer, and only grace will open the heavens for artists to sing with purpose. "But this is not the end, Babette. I'm certain it's not." Filippa's words and resolute expression offer a soft rebuke to any hint of vanity remaining in the beloved cook, for Filippa has played all the way through a similar set of cards. Human martyrdom and sacrifice have little purpose unless placed in the largest of all contexts—without the resurrection, we are the fools of the world, reminds St. Paul. The General's tender words to Martine are not enough, for though he will carry her in his soul, she remains on the earth as a body and soul together subject to the slow clock of cruel time. That was the point of the feast after all. We exist soul and body, suffer soul and body, exult soul and body. In this life Martine will remain alone in the cool, evening sheets while her knight errant rides boldly into his remaining adventures. For the affair to be a divine comedy, the lovers must one day reunite. So also, with Filippa's vocal artistry. Her sweet voice must indeed delight the angels and the saints in eternal time or her reconciliation with the memory of Papin is little more than sentiment.

*Babette's Feast* plays out a Eucharist more than anything. The saints remember their slain king and Lord but also await a consummation, a return where they will sit before a sumptuous meal and eat. When Christ appeared after the resurrection, he sat with his disciples, and they had another supper, according to the Scriptures. It was not Babette who directed the reconciliations that redeem the story. She did not bring Papin to the sisters; nor was it her free resolve to follow his lead to the Jutland. She did not bring Löwenhielm back into the story to reunite with Martine. Babette did not surround the village with the great sea, nor color the sky so beautifully around it. She did not bring the stars low to bless the poor singers, so earnest yet so shrunken by the small-minded tyranny of their indomitable minister. Babette was simply a messenger of the new covenant. She brought the meal but was not the meal. She fulfilled her call as artist to reveal the true artist who alone can weave together the words that describe our stories.

Christ comes through the bread and wine in the consummate liturgical celebration. Moreover, believers are reminded of his long-awaited future arrival through the meanderings of providence that tend always to lead forward, not back. When the General peers into Martine's eyes and assures her of his undying spiritual devotion, we feel our own distinct tug and pull of perfect love and perfect heaven. We recall with a deeper ache how grace has operated the slow motions of that love and heaven rolling through our sad days. We recall those spots of time when the stars seemed closer to us, when a smiling Christ cast benevolent eyes our way with the message, I saw outcast Hagar and as I saw Nathaniel under the tree and I see you. Just wait, only wait. These latter words recall the bittersweet end of Chekhov's *Uncle Vanya* when the doomsayer playwright blessed the mouth of the most worthy and saintly player, the sorrowing daughter of that work's tragic events, Sonya: "We shall rest. We shall hear the angels. We shall see heaven shining like a jewel. We shall see all evil and all our pain sink away in the great compassion that shall enfold the world. Our life will be as peaceful and tender and sweet as a caress. I have faith; I have faith."

Such hopeful reflections get stirred by this wonderful film. Love has become incarnate before us in the experience of all three women who sacrificed and then gained more—Martine who hears Löwenhielm express his final devotion in the hall, Filippa who hears read the letter from Papin and grasps hold of Babette, now her other sister, and Babette herself gazing off screen at the rainbow arc of her own life. We are moved as by the warmth of the sun on an early spring morning turned to momentary grief by the trail of shadows from passing clouds.

It was late on a weeknight. Our youngest son, who does not see the world well, our dear, adopted son graced without common comprehension and its adjoining warnings, our son who had so wanted a car to be free to do whatever, who had worked two part-time jobs and spent not a penny to save up for more than a year—our beloved son limped into the bedroom to tell us he had slammed that car into the side wall of the downtown tunnel having taken a turn in the rain driving three times too fast. He pinballed two hundred yards off those concrete walls, the officer told him. A friend who rode shotgun fortunately only got a broken nose, our son said, and as for him, he only strained his neck and back. The car was totaled, but nothing else. No other cars. No other passengers. It was his fault and he admitted it without hesitation, and he knew he wouldn't be driving again anytime soon. He had no car now nor money, and he was shaken, but okay. He understood that friends would no longer call for his rent-a-driver service.

And here is the point of that. In the strange and kindly providence of heaven, our smiling Lord gave us an improbable gift with that late-night visit from our impossible-to-understand son. God answered in the most unexpected way our many nightly prayers for Isaac's protection following his purchase of that car.

We all have such stories. There is a mercy that guides us in mysterious and beautiful ways, as old Cowper wrote,

*Judge not the Lord by feeble sense,*
*but trust Him for His grace;*
*behind a frowning providence*
*He hides a smiling face.*

We would have more faith and hope, but we tend to fret our own insignificance. That is also a truth visible along the edge of *Babette's Feast*, the nagging stone in the shoe of our daily journeying. *Why should our little affairs matter after all?* The insistence of the evil question tempts us.

The film opens with the two young women walking to town side by side, beautiful but austere, their stories introduced with an impassive voiceover, the trademark of a tale caught in a rigid fatality. We are told how few their prospects of love now are, though they are so very lovely. They live in a grey village under the cold spell of its own white witch. It is winter forever in the village. The church has become a captured enterprise, the hobby world of a selfish demigod. These daughters exist only to serve his narrative, the other congregants to celebrate his themes. Who can break the spell? Who will care enough to even try in this remote, dream kingdom of death?

Such is the gnawing emptiness that Papin felt when he first arrived in the Jutland. He walked across the hills above the village and beheld the vast, silent sea, and realized that all the dazzle of his Parisienne world masked an ugly face. He himself would one day be replaced on the stage and forgotten. Time would wash away his songs and likely mock them. He had become the exemplar of the fate the older General Löwenhielm tossed in the face of his impassive, younger self, and as such he had become the captive hearer of the bittersweet song of eternal wisdom:

> *What does it matter after all? Why all this striving?*
> *The sun rises, and the sun goes down,*
> *and hastens*[1] *to the place where it rises.*
> *The wind blows to the south*
> *and goes around to the north;*
> *around and around goes the wind,*
> *and on its circuits the wind returns.*
> *All streams run to the sea,*
> *but the sea is not full;*
> *to the place where the streams flow,*
> *there they flow again.*
> *All things are full of weariness;*
> *a man cannot utter it;*
> *the eye is not satisfied with seeing,*
> *nor the ear filled with hearing.*
> *What has been is what will be,*
> *and what has been done is what will be done,*
> *and there is nothing new under the sun.*
>
> Ecclesiastes 1: 5-9

But there is more, Babette. This cannot be all. No, it is not all, for the face of Christ smiles even from that place of most exquisite suffering.

# 5
# THE NATURAL

> *AND And ther was he sworn unto his lordes and the comyns for to be a true kyng, to stand with true justyce fro thensforth the dayes of this lyf. Also thenne he made alle lordes that helde of the croune to come in and to do servyce as they oughte to doo.*
>
> —Thomas Malory, *Le Morte D'Arthur*

The fate of the community awaits the coming true king; the rest of politics be damned.

For a portrait of that royal deliverer, consider briefly the life of Samson. One of Israel's more memorable judges who ruled after Moses and prior to the establishment of the Davidic monarchy, Samson was appointed by God to deliver the Jews from the oppression of the barbarous Philistines who occupied lands along the coast of the Mediterranean northwest of the Promised Land.

The story begins when an angel appears to Samson's mother and informs her that though barren, she will bear a son, a familiar redemptive motif, and that her son is to be dedicated to God as a Nazirite, drinking no wine and with his hair left uncut for life. The parents obey, and as accessory to this divine appointment, Samson is given superhuman ability, which he uses well to terrify Israel's enemies. Sadly, Samson also possesses a more than healthy libido and a poor understanding of the sixth commandment. When he finally marries, it is to a Philistine woman, Delilah, who is leveraged by the military leaders of her native land to discover the source of Samson's remarkable strength. Eventually broken down by her seductions, Samson tells Delilah that the power came with his Nazirite vow, and if someone were to cut his hair, the Spirit would depart him. She sells him out, of course, and Philistine hit men play barber while he sleeps and cart him off. Samson is then blinded and paraded out periodically for the amusement of the enemy rulers who exult in what they perceive to be a sign of the ultimate victory of their god Dagon. They weren't paying close attention to the story, however, and when Samson's hair grows back in prison, his strength begins to return and he repents and prays for one last burst to pull down the pillars of the Philistine temple upon the heads of a large gathering of leading men and observant fools there to watch him humiliated one more time. The Lord hears and Samson kills more of the oppressors in his final, self-sacrificial act than he had in his lifetime before,

> *And Samson said, "Let me die with the Philistines." Then he bowed with all his strength, and the house fell upon the lords and upon all the people who were in it. So the dead whom he killed at his death were more than those whom he had killed during his life. (Judges 16: 30)*

The heroic structure of the account is simple to outline. The people favored by God have been sorely oppressed by an evil force. In response to their cries for help, God appoints a hero whom He endows with extraordinary power. The hero's gift is rooted in personal integrity connected to a sacramental element, Samson's hair in the biblical narrative. While in full possession of his power, the hero rallies an oppressed minority and provides deliverance through a series of extraordinary deeds in battle. The hero is not Christ, though prefiguring that one who would come to be king, because this earthly hero has faults, and in time, temptation, often sexual, causes him a temporary fall and loss of the sacramental. As result of that collapse, the people suffer again at the hands of their oppressors. Then follows the hero's repentance and the sacramental restoration after which he accomplishes an unprecedented feat which leads the suffering people to a great deliverance.

The pattern recurs throughout the Old Testament and in the lives of the saints and is echoed during significant events through Christian history, such as the Battle of Lepanto in 1571. The heroic storyline leads to a miraculous resurrection and ascension, the divine victory that exemplifies the rewards of purity, providing a heritage that realizes the paradoxical truth embedded in the famous line of Tertullian in his *Apologeticus* written near the end of the second century, "The blood of the martyrs is the seed of the church." Out of seeming ignominious death and defeat arises a new strength and greater victory. Christ's life is the prototype, differing only as he is the one hero who never yields to temptation, though sorely tried; the passion that concludes his mortal life being the consequence of the failure of the people whom he represents.

In the fictional narrative tradition of the West, the elements of the Biblical heroic pattern are most vividly expressed in the tales of the chivalrous Arthurian knights, in particular Thomas Malory's great fifteenth-century rendering of those tales in the epic *Le Morte D'Arthur.* The distinction in Malory is that his Arthurian rendition ends still anticipating the final salvific victory—Mordred has delivered Arthur a mortal wound, and three queens take him by barge to the land of Avalon, his magical sword Excalibur given to Sir Bedivere who throws it back to the Lady of the Lake. Then, in his conclusion, Malory suggests that Arthur may come again as king to provide a final restoration,

> *Yet some men say in many parts of England that King Arthur is not dead, but had by the will of our Lord Jesu into another place; and men say that he shall come again, and he shall win the holy cross.*

This eschatological component likely came through the twelfth-century sources that Malory used, sources reflecting the developing scholastic theology of the late Middle Ages which better aligned the material with the Christology of the Biblical accounts, the life and death of one great judge prefiguring a still greater judge until the final return of the king.

The Arthurian pattern in Malory, whose rendition has proven most influential in the legend's influence, synthesizes what can be found in accounts like that of Samson in the Book of Judges with what is detailed in the Gospels. The hero is flawed as in the story of Samson; yet, he will achieve a permanent victory in due time as did Christ. One additional story element is layered in. The rise of Camelot in the Arthurian tales follows Arthur's special appointment, signified by his ability in a public ceremony to draw the magic sword Excalibur from the stone which appears in a cathedral churchyard in London on Christmas Eve. Arthur's acceptance to head his Round Table of fellowship depends on God alone designating him publicly as the rightful king. His prosperous reign of harmony ends only after a direct assault on the holiness of this entire enterprise; that being when Arthur's best knight, Lancelot, commits adultery with the queen, Guinevere. This adultery, which Arthur has tolerated to a degree, echoes two Old Testament accounts regarding King David—his own adultery with Bathsheba and then his betrayal by his son Absalom who will publicly debauch all David's wives and concubines to kick off his rebellion. The violation of the terms of the kingly appointment through these "grievous" mortal sins triggers the climactic acts in the legend, first the failed grail quest and then the civil war under Arthur's bastard son Mordred which leads to Arthur's mortal wound. So, deep under the more commonly known details of the Arthurian legend hides at the core this sacramental reality: the appointed king who holds together the community governs that *fragile* community only through the means of a *fragile* personal integrity securing a wavering grip on a divine covenant.

The elements of this legend have spread through much subsequent written and visual literature and especially popular literature in the West, from the more cerebral Arthur Conan Doyle stories featuring Sherlock Holmes to the romantic stories of the American West first described by the pen of James Fenimore Cooper in his *Leatherstocking Tales* to space-exploration franchise films like *Star Wars* to the visceral *Rocky*-styled "shepherd to king" films and later to the Marvel and DC superhero films. The appointed hero protects the oppressed minority through an exceptional power linked to personal integrity through a sacramental covenant. Temptation and temporary fall, restoration and glorious victory, and through it all, the impossible-to-miss fragility of the hero as well as the threatened people.

Barry Levinson's 1984 classic *The Natural* can be best appreciated within this context. To recognize the alignment, all one need do is read a plot summary—Roy Hobbs joins the struggling, rag-tag New York Knights and proves a phenomenal slugger who leads them to an improbable pennant against the bad will of a corrupt owner in cahoots with a gambler. The evil agents will try, almost successfully, to corrupt Hobbs with the intention that he throws the final game and the team loses while the money barons and criminals win, a story idea obviously picked up from the famous 1919 Black Sox scandal in major league baseball. Hobbs' temporary moral fall results from a sexual temptation; in fact, he seems as vulnerable as Samson in this arena. Also like Samson, he eventually repents the folly and rises again in the final game to hit a prodigious home run that wins the Knights the pennant to the joy of the manager Pop, the underdog players, and young Knights' fans all over the country praying for their hero to save the team.

Two observations to start. First, what Clive Bell termed significant form is clearly inherent in the archetypal story pattern described above. The biblical hero story taps into a longing deep within the human spirit, especially in cultures formed further by the Judeo-Christian tradition. No matter how many times the familiar story structure is realized, the audience reacts approvingly when the execution of that story is artful. Second and related, the resonance of *The Natural* in popular culture, now across more than three decades, suggests something even better captured in this film than numerous others of similar content produced over the same span, many involving sport.

Underneath the archetypal hero-savior motif—call it Arthurian for simplicity—lies an appeal to those central longings for love and heaven. The fact that a hero is appointed and sent to a specific community implies a benevolent providence concerned for the well-being of that community. Long before Roy Hobbs climbs up the ramp and into the Knights dugout, the story suggests that the plight of Pop and his struggling team has invited divine sympathy. Though the film purports to be about the deliverer, "the Natural," it is more about the people longing for deliverance. By the time the credits roll, Roy has himself been folded back into the community as a redeemed subject. Divine sympathy has responded to humans longing, "thy kingdom come, thy will be done on earth as it is in heaven." The source of this divine sympathy is love, and the sending of the deliverer is grace birthed in love. The objects of that gift request and find mercy. The film moves the emotions principally through the pull of this familiar story pattern that speaks the hope that what is played in fiction will be played in difficult personal realities. One might go further in the argument to say that the universal response to the film's hero message confirms that hearts are indeed tuned for that message; in other words, the viewers are tuned to place personal hope in a heroic savior because they are made for that salvation. The significant form is significant because as St. Augustine famously prayed, "Our hearts are restless until they rest in thee."

The film's agreement with these older voices depends on a key alteration writers Phil Dusenberry and Roger Towne brought to their screenplay from the original novel by Bernard Malamud. In the Malamud novel, Hobbs capitulates to the mob and strikes out in his last at bat to the dismay of all those desperate Knights' fans; the conclusion to the novel is thus bitterly ironic and anticlimactic. In the film, however, Hobbs repents of his early mistakes, the temptations for money and pleasure, and rises from a hospital bed—in a maternity ward no less—to homer off the light tower. His mighty blow rains sparks of light upon the celebrants on the field and in the stands. The sequence then transitions into an iconic image of Hobbs playing catch with his son in a wheat field with his beloved wife looking on, a romantic portrait worthy of Willa Cather and Thomas Cole—heaven as imagined through rural American in a more pristine age.

Few films are as coherent in conception as *The Natural*, nor as tightly designed. No opportunity is wasted by Levinson and his editors to reinforce the themes through visual or auditory cues. The narrative unfolds as a sequence of mirrored vignettes: point and counterpoint bookends from start to finish. The first bookends are the opening and closing scenes on the farm, first with Roy and his father playing ball and last with wife Iris watching Roy play catch with his son. Next inside that frame is the scene establishing Roy's pitching prowess in a contest with The Whammer, a Babe Ruth type whom Roy strikes out in three pitches at a county fair, that matches the film's penultimate scene in which Roy turns around and plays the role of the Whammer hitting his game-winning home run against a Nebraska farm boy with a blazing fastball and sun-bleached blonde hair like his own. In between those are two more mirrored scenes—Roy shot in a hotel room by Harriet Bird, a femme fatale he meets on the train headed to Chicago, to Roy nearly shot in the Judge's office by Memo Paris, the other femme fatale, the Delilah who leads Roy through sex to his temporary loss of grace. Inside that pairing are two montage sequences, one at the beginning with Roy establishing the Knights as contenders through game-by-game heroics to Roy returning the team to contention through a new set of heroics after his slump. And so it goes, the story progress like the opening of Matryoshka nesting dolls.

The Knights' resurrection from the ashes, and near return to those same ashes, reflects the arc of Roy's own story—his arrival and success to Memo's honey pot temptation to a period of failure and near despair prior to victory. A further mirror is that Memo the temptress is Pop the manager's fallen angel daughter who has been corrupted by Gus, the gambler working alongside the Judge, the owner and banker. So, the good people are threatened by a wasteland curse with Memo the primary carrier of blight. Her hair is blonde as is Iris' hair, but dyed that way as she is a faux damsel; her bright, red nails link her to Harriet Bird who seduced Roy on the train and lured him to her hotel room where she waited in funeral garb to execute him and then commit suicide. Memo turns to Roy after her former love, Bump, dies crashing through a fence chasing a flyball while trying to win back the starting job Roy took from him. Later in the film it is suggested she might just as easily next slide from Roy to the team's pitcher, Al, also under a bribe to satisfy one of Gus' wagers. Memo connects with Roy at a party run by Gus and takes him out to a private place to consummate the affair, spinning her web as a spider will do under a dock; she then poisons Roy at a party run by Gus to keep him from playing in the final game. Under her spell, Roy can no longer hit the baseball, and the team loses. Roy had been warned by Pop on a couple of occasions that Memo is bad luck. She is indeed, weaving a Delilah-like spell that cuts off the hero's hair, so to speak, and renders him powerless at the plate.

Memo's spell is broken by the intercession of the virtuous woman, Roy's childhood sweetheart Iris. Roy's prowess had been connected to Iris from the start of the story. In the initial scene she is a little girl watching him play ball with his father; she later, unbeknownst to him until the end, becomes the mother of his child after giving herself to him freely in the family barn before Roy leaves to try out in Chicago. Aligned with Iris is Roy's bat, Wonderboy, carved from an oak on the family land under which his father died of a heart attack. The oak was split by a lightning bolt, a heavenly sign of divine power and grace that renders the bat a sacramental. Lightning will flash prior to Roy's final home run as a sign of the return of his power, as it does when Iris first returns to watch him play and he responds by breaking the scoreboard at Wrigley Field with a home run.

Placed in the larger Christian context, the name Iris suggests clarity of vision, both the flower and the center of the eye, while etymologically it derives from the Greek word for rainbow, a suggestion of divine grace. She is clothed in white with the sun shining behind her when she stands to cheer Roy out of his slump in Chicago, his original destination before Harriet intercepted him. That iconography makes plain that she stands behind him as a true inspiration, unlike Memo. Iris returns to Roy's life as the new Eve who replaces the corrupted Eve. As their son was conceived in a barn, Iris is a further echo of the Madonna, the dispenser of the vision that leads the lost wanderer from the dark woods back to the path ending in the beatific vision. Twice Iris sends Roy letters that clarify the details of his life story in order to return him to his redemptive calling. Once she writes to tell him she is in town for one of his games, the day she will rise in the crowd to inspire his scoreboard-breaking home run. Then at the end she writes to let Roy know her son, his son, is in the stands watching the championship game, a revelation which restores Roy's power and leads to the mighty, light-tower blow.

In mirror contrast to Iris' letters of guidance are the sketches and articles of the journalist Max Mercy who has followed Roy's career, and who becomes the bent instrument used by the mob to tell the public "the truth" of Roy's sordid past, the hotel room exploit with Harriet that ruined his career as a pitcher and led to his return to the game only after an impossible sixteen years. Mercy's jaded story of Roy's past is used by Gus and the Judge to reinforce their final bribe, the threat being that if Roy does not comply with their demands, such a story would corrupt the youth who have come to idolize the slugger. Iris' letters pull Roy back to a version of his life grounded in heroic love. Mercy, ironically named, tries to reshape Roy's story into a narrative that justifies his own cynicism and feeds the corrupt interests of the financial underworld behind the game.

This central moral tension in the story derives from the conventional contrast of innocent country life against corrupt city life. However, it speaks beyond that to a central problem of modernity, the loss of belief in absolutes and the corresponding replacement of ideals with constructed fictions. What is truth, Pilate asked in the throes of his own despair, the question hovering in the air over nineteenth- and early twentieth-century intellectuals. Mercy brings the question to Roy in a conversation late in the film as they walk in the shadows of a bridge. He warns of the consequence of his publishing of Roy's back story, insisting that the journalist's role is to create what people think about players like Roy who come and go. An argument on Mercy's side presented directly to the film viewer is in the newspaper headlines used throughout the film as transitional devices, "fictions" created to form the public mind in regard to the plight of the team and Roy's connection to it, both for good and ill.

One might block the formal elements of the plot into a another set of contrasts. On one side would be the satanic Judge who keeps his office lights off to defy his fear of the dark, the pragmatic gambler Gus with his one glass eye, and Memo, the captured woman who straddles both sides but proves her damnation in the end by poisoning Roy. Harriet might be added, damned as well when she enters the story. Associated themes would be the deadly sins of pride, avarice, sexual license, deception, and betrayal. Associated motifs would be darkness, physical distance, and blood. In counterpoint to all of these would be the good-hearted Iris with Pop and his loyal assistant Red. The contrary themes would be humility, simplicity, domesticity, honesty, and loyalty. Contrary motifs would be purity, light, and community.

The characters who totter between the two forces are Roy and in a dimmer reflection Al, star pitcher on the Knights also under the influence of the mob. Other characters seem fixed in their moral positions. Again, what pulls Roy and with him Al back toward virtue is the mediation of the woman Iris. She enters the conflict from the outside and offers the wisdom and grace needed for Roy to overcome his temptation. As Roy lies in the hospital bed trying to decide if he will play in the last game, she offers him the path to redemption through a choice, "I believe we have two lives… the life we learn with and the life we live with after that." Roy can choose to give in to the cynical fatalism of Max Mercy or he can choose to learn from and reverse his mistakes and live a penitential and redemptive life. Iris presents the offer and then stands with him and his son in the conclusion once he has made the right choice.

The fragile community at stake in the conflict is as important as these central characters. Iris suggests as much, reminding Roy that his victory will also be the victory of his son. "A boy needs a father," Roy agrees. It was the absence of Roy's own father that contributed to his collapse, the loss of a wise guide warning him about the dangers ahead. Roy's fatal flaw has been naiveté born of familial loss. He did not see it coming with Harriet, he says, nor with Memo, though he should have known better with Memo. Even with the Judge and Gus and Mercy he is a half-step behind until the very end. Pop is a surrogate father, and Roy acknowledges in the end that he is also playing the final game to give Pop the pennant he longs for, as well as releasing Pop from a bad contract with the Judge that would lead him to ruin. Pop counsels Roy throughout, and though Roy does not always listen, their relationship evolves. Pop always wanted to be a farmer, he tells Roy in the very moving climactic scene in the clubhouse upon Roy's return for the final game. Roy confirms, "Nothing like a farm. Nothing like being around animals. Fixing things. Nothing like being in a field by yourself, the vegetables and the corn, the winter wheat, the greenest stuff you ever saw"; but, implied in his words, better still is the smell of the green grass of the outfield and the dirt of the bullpen and the feel of the soft arc of the pitcher's mound. "Suit up," Pop tells Roy, commissioning him as his real father had at the start in words that again echo something biblical: King David, confronted with the threat of the belligerent fool Nabal, commanding his men, "Strap on your swords."

Beyond Roy and the Knights players, and Pop and Red, the stakeholders are the fan base, the young boys who watch the games with their fathers and other family members, often the principal subjects for the camera through the action sequences. They cheer on their heroes and, we assume, find vicariously the courage to face their own challenges. The idea is introduced in Roy's contest against the Whammer, when a young boy who has seen Roy strike the Whammer out in three pitches runs to him for an autograph before Roy gets back on the train. The boy needs a hero, and Roy has drawn the sword from the stone and supplanted the Whammer in that role.

Stand-in for all the young hopefuls is the Knights' batboy Bobby Savoy. Roy's on-field deeds are most often recorded through his reactions. Bobby is on the field watching when Roy first arrives with his contract to play for the Knights. We see Roy's first batting session through his eyes. Bobby is invariably framed in shots where Roy's iconic stature is at stake. It is Bobby who provides Roy the magic sword that wins the final day, the replacement bat they made together one fine afternoon, the Savoy Special. Roy uses the Savoy Special to launch his pennant-clinching homerun. In an iconic moment, he hands Roy the magic bat after Roy's "Wonderboy" has broken, and the two smile warmly, knowingly, as light bulbs to record the coming great deed, framing the moment for all lovers of the game who will follow and remember the great Roy Hobbs. The image of the two sharing a dream rebuts Max Mercy's cynicism; the dream is the truth after all. Bobby's reaction of awe and delight mirrors that of the film viewer also celebrating as Roy rounds the bases after winning the pennant for Pop and the team. It is what the film has been all about. Pop's expression in the same sequence contains less awe than shock that his curse has been broken, he too long under it and now grown old. But not Bobby. Bobby is forever young and vulnerable and innocent. He stands for young boys who dream of playing in the game and hitting a long one, the boys who collect and trade cards and cry softly in the living room before the television set when the key game is lost and hopes dashed.

It is the character of Bobby who makes *The Natural* so personal, and who is central to its significant form. Children old enough to appreciate a game like baseball, and not yet jaded by too soon an entrance into the world outside the game, a condition represented through Max Mercy, do look at their favorite players with a kind of reverent awe. In the heaven of a boy's mind as he waits through the long days prior to manhood, there exists the dream of a divine providence that will work for good, somehow. The troubles of the day can be corrected by a well-placed bunt or a sneaky curve on the outer edge in the next game or the next season. Should Malamud's version of the story been taken to screen, the story would have championed Max's version of reality at the expense of Bobby, hardly fair since Bobby is an innocent with choices ahead of him, whereas Max can no longer avoid being anything other than the jaded cynic.

In *What Is Art?* Leo Tolstoy asserts that the infectiousness of a work belongs within the domain of a universal religious perception which Tolstoy insists has guided every civilization: "All history shows that the progress of humanity is accomplished not otherwise than under the guidance of religion." And he goes further to define the Christian perception of art "in the recognition by every man of his sonship to God, and of the consequent union of men with God and with one another."[12] He saw this as the heart of the gospel.

One may quibble over Tolstoy's rigidity in determining which works of art unite and which divide; yet, his principles are hard to dispute given what is found in a film like *The Natural*, centered as it is on the bringing to harmony a man and his world and the consequent union of all those in loving relation with him. Roy Hobbs becomes the savior of all the innocents and unlikely souls around him. As Iris suggests Mary, Roy with his natural grace and bloody uniform suggests Christ, especially in his triumphant final at bat, and such interpretations are in step with the heroic tradition discussed at the start of this chapter. It is no accident of staging that as Iris walks into the maternity suite where Roy convalesces after his poisoning, a crucifix graces the wall of the room alongside her in the camera frame. Roy Hobbs stands in that peculiar line of fictional heroes of which the world of readers is not worthy, to borrow from the writer of Hebrews.

And this all leads to a final point. It would be easy to go on to describe all the various devices the film employs to underscore theme and character arc—elevators going up and down, *film noir* blinds, the manipulation of light and shadow, and, most notably, the rich musical score accompanying the action, a score echoing Aaron Copland and so evocative of an older, now lost America. Those are significant matters of form, and there are others. However, it seems more appropriate to conclude this chapter by addressing the higher subject of religious art. Tradition makes clear that the earliest impulse of Christian iconography was sacramental. Paintings of the Lord and Lady and the saints from the earliest centuries of the Church pulled the worshipper into the experience of the Incarnation and Passion stories. Fourteen centuries passed before the Renaissance steered Western art a hard left turn toward the purely representational; that is, the fascination of human possibility and the exalted role of the artist. For many centuries the Host was the great icon of the Church, on display in a gilded monstrance for Adoration during certain hours and seasons so that the devout might contemplate Christ and receive grace through a devotional exercise. For centuries, art followed the lead of liturgical practice from iconography to the design of cathedrals. Beautiful religious artifacts were not sacraments, but sacramentals, physical objects that transmitted blessings from heaven.

The Christian epic form that found its way through the chivalric tales of writers like Chrétien de Troyes in France and Thomas Malory in England was built upon this sacramental foundation. Malory's *Morte D'Arthur* is a Passion tale in which a reader wanders from an earthly paradise through events colored by the infectious consequences of sin through a bloody pilgrimage in pursuit of the holy to the death of the hero and promise of a restored world to come. Earlier works such as *The Dream of the Rood* had established the pattern: a soldier of Christ contemplates the sacrifice of Christ through a narrative told by the tree that carried Christ, the reader allowed to join in the Passion story through the sacramental narrative and thus engage the hero of the Passion with immediacy.

As will be taken up in later chapters, when filmmakers reach for ways to display moments of transcendence in works directed toward religious perceptions, they typically alter the style of their films to cue the viewer. So, in *The Natural* the filmmaking style shifts in the scenes when ordinary objects and character icons become sacramentals. The music changes key, the screen explodes with new color or brightness, and the narrative clock slows dramatically. Roy's homerun ball becomes the ball he throws his son in the wheat field, travelling a slow-motion arc through a now bright blue, not jet black, sky. The flight of the ball becomes emblem of grace, divine intervention like a rainbow reconnecting both parts of a broken world.

Film narratives that follow along these lines trace back history to two fundamental conceptions, the incarnation of Jesus Christ and the bloody sacrifice of love at the Lord's death: Bethlehem and Calvary. The Faith demands both, as in Bethlehem God became man through the womb of a virgin and so entered the valley of sorrows, and at Calvary Christ poured out his blood to purchase the salvation of his people.

The thunderbolt that splits the tree from which Roy's original weapon Wonderboy is taken splits the sky in two other scenes when deeds of unearthly power redeem the day. It becomes the image the Knights take for an arm badge, an image that signals the entrance of the Divine into the Bethlehem of the flesh. Roy's hard pilgrimage leads him into direct confrontation with the Judge and the gambler Gus, through his poisoning by Memo to the hospital bed to his last at bat, his Passion—it will be his very last at bat. The camera notes the bloody wound on Roy's side just prior to his great home run.

This sacramentalism in *The Natural* does not depend on what Malamud or Levinson, both Jewish, or their screenwriters believed about these matters or what the actors and technical professionals even understood—the elements came through the source materials and so through the traditions of the Catholic faith. Like a baptism delivered by a nonbelieving priest to nonbelieving parents, the sacrament is still valid if the formula is followed because of the deeper waters of grace running strong underneath. And that grace gets imparted to those taken up into the story.

In the early scene in Chicago when Iris stands and Roy breaks his slump and the scoreboard, to the climactic sequence when he homers to win the pennant and then tosses a ball to his son on the farm, something magical takes place *beyond* the screen. A measure of grace is offered to all who watch with faith. Roy's exploits affirm that the iconic divine deliverer inspired by the holy lady will come to succor the humble of heart. And as these patterns are conjured from the realm of the real and not from pure imagination, the film viewer does indeed feel the tug of that other place. We have longed for just such a triumphal deliverance, whether baseball fans or not. And our longed-for deliverance is not soteriological, a rescue from sin's pursuit, it is romantic, the release from the corruptions of the world that have imprisoned joy into the freshness of our most cherished visions.

# 6
# ROCKY

> *The young warrior stripped himself then—that was God Almighty—strong and firm of purpose—he climbed up onto the high gallows, magnificent in the sight of many.*
>
> —The Dream of the Rood

"You want to leave some footprints on the canvas of life, and they don't have to be big ones. Everyone doesn't have to be a world champion. Just the fact that you gave it your best. That's the Rocky philosophy. He never expected to be champion. He just wanted to go the distance and have a little dignity. And that's pretty much the ongoing theme." The words of Sylvester Stallone, the man who would seemingly know best what runs through the veins of the 1976 Academy Award winner *Rocky* as he both wrote the original screenplay and starred as the journeyman who got a dream shot to fight the heavyweight champion of the world, Apollo Creed. And these words came from an older, more reflective Sylvester Stallone in a New Line Cinema promo for *Creed II,* a 2018 sequel within the lucrative *Rocky* franchise.

In a series of media interviews around years 2013-2014, Stallone acknowledged that the title character is a Christian crusader who sacrificed himself for the good of others. The admission was quite personal, as Stallone himself had recently come back to the Catholic faith after in his words "losing his way" upon arrival in Hollywood. Given how the *Rocky* films all aim toward a ritualistic, violent final event in the ring, this alignment with matters of faith and devotion may raise questions for casual observers, but there it is.

At the very least, all should agree that *Rocky* is about human dignity, and in the context of the Christian understanding of man created in the *imago Dei*—that is, man as a creature made in God's likeness to be known and loved and given a name worth repeating, to be prepared for heaven.

John Paul II in his 1995 encyclical *Evangelium Vitae* wrote, "The sacredness of life gives rise to its inviolability, written from the beginning in man's heart, in his conscience." When our innate condition is affirmed by birth and life circumstance, what follows is typically a life of purpose and confidence. When denied and attacked, what may result is a life of insecurity, despair, and potential suicide, the ultimate denial. Our greatest internal inspiration may in fact be beaten into hard doubt through hard experience. The power of the film *Rocky* resides in the tension between these two possibilities. The title character's internal confidence is tottering, an event most of us can understand as we reflect upon our psychological development. However, rather than have the story unravel in the way of modern existentialism, the film concludes by affirming the dignity of the small man, and, in particular, the small man challenged to the breaking point by the compromises and betrayals of a claustrophobic, urban existence. It is a film and franchise about human triumph over the despair created from grinding, endemic disappointment and dehumanization. As such *Rocky* addressed a growing population in America and across the globe caught in the web of that same modern enterprise, and so it brought applause, accolades, and tears. Stallone had tapped into something deeply human and deeply relevant; the film was produced on a one-million-dollar budget and went on to earn 225 million and spark a franchise and others related, like the *Karate Kid* films.

The script behind the film was inspired by the famous 1975 heavyweight championship fight between Muhammed Ali and journeyman Chuck Wepner. Ali had just come off the Rumble in the Jungle victory over George Foreman in Zaire and Wepner off a loss to the aged Sonny Liston who beat Wepner so badly that he required 120 stitches afterward. Despite the odds, Wepner lasted fifteen rounds with Ali, even knocking him down with a body punch in the ninth round. Stallone, watching the fight at home, saw a reflection of himself, his film career sputtering, and that Ali/Wepner fight became the creative inspiration for his original script—a Cinderella story of a seemingly clumsy underdog white fighter against a brash black champion. The Catholicism of Stallone's Italian upbringing baked itself into the Cinderella tale as well.

Early in my career I received a bad book review from an academic who could see no grounds for discussing a film like *Rocky* in the same pages as discussions of films like *Babette's Feast* or Murnau's *Sunrise.* The objection was grounded in two common assumptions; first, that a popular film that spins off a long series of sequels cannot be taken seriously, and second, that a stylistically limited film cannot evoke the kind of transcendent response this book means to address. To the first objection, lovers of literature ought to recall that *Henry IV*, *The Hobbit*, and *Don Quixote* all fit that description of the popular. In fact, despite modern insistence to the contrary, the history of letters tells the tale that the best of literature has been passed on simply because it is the best *kind* to pass on. It is of that universal kind that speaks across barriers. To the second objection regarding the stylistic limitations of the film *Rocky*, those who have been paying attention to the argument of this book should note the missed premise—those deep matters which move us most dwell in a realm beyond the words on a page or images on the screen.

One other point should be made to begin. When we discuss the religious, that is Christian, elements of a film, we speak about the deep narrative structures at work. The most profound influence of Christianity on international film form and content has been the liturgical tradition of the Church which offers the mass as a reenactment of Calvary. First comes the declaration of condemnation and forgiveness, then the covenantal texts of the epistles and gospel, then the consecration and reception. When the host is transformed, the liturgy moves us through matters of human comprehension to a miracle of God. That is, our participation in that liturgy culminates in the non-rational yet so very tangible eating of the transformed presence of the Savior of the world. At some moment in typical religious films informed by the Western tradition, God likewise enters the story and the substance of the narrative elements is transformed: the story is redeemed and lives differently afterward. One can find the pattern in the most sublime of films like *Andre Rublev*, *The Diary of a Country Priest*, or *The Passion of Joan of Arc*; and one can find it in vehicles as easy on the mind as *It's a Wonderful Life*, *The Wizard of Oz*, or, yes, *Rocky*.

*Rocky* begins by invoking the most profound of Catholic symbols, the Eucharist. The setting is a low-end boxing club apparently located in a church where Rocky is matched against a journeyman fighter in what seems more a wrestling match than boxing. The camera begins the story above the ring with a large image of Christ holding a consecrated host over a chalice. It pauses there then tracks back and down to the church name, "Resurrection A. C." Then we move to the fighters. Rocky is taking punishment and so is aligned immediately with the suffering Christ; however, that opening image was not of the crucifix but of a triumphant Christ, and the contrast serves to tip the film viewer to the direction the story will go. Rocky will somehow turn this around. By contrast, the masses at ringside in the fiction take in both the sufferer and the triumphal savior overhead, but they are at present disconnected in consciousness from both. A woman in the crowd stands and yells, "C'mon, hit him, hit him," an invective reminiscent of the guillotine women in Dickens' *A Tale of Two Cities.* And indeed, the fight takes an ugly turn as Spider Rico headbutts Rocky cutting him above the eye. That bit of chicanery in another foreshadowing awakens Rocky's shrunken competitive nature, and he responds to the cheap shot by pounding Rico into the canvas.

The iconography of the scene establishes the basic premise, as well as offering a visual, thematic context. The blood from Rocky's cut eye will be mirrored in much more pronounced fashion during his fight with Creed, when to come out for the final round Rocky will ask his trainer Mick to cut him to reduce the swelling above the eye so that he can see and continue fighting. In the arc of his story Rocky moves from the purposeless bloodshed of the opening match with Spider Rico to freely offered blood at the end. Thematically, once Rocky is transformed, his blood redeems himself and all the other lost souls like him who participate in the ritual vicariously.

In similar fashion, prominent in Rocky's apartment is the cross on the shelf over his bed, which creates a visual center point for a later conversation between Rocky and his girlfriend Adrian when he announces he can't beat Creed but would prove himself a someone if he could at least go the distance. To further this, the film is set in early winter between Thanksgiving and Christmas. Rocky's courtship of Adrian strides those two winter feasts. Snow falls from heaven as Rocky trains for the big fight, suggesting how grace redeems the winter despair. Before meeting Creed in the ring, Rocky kneels at the sink in the locker room in prayer. When Rocky is knocked to the canvas near the fight's end, Adrian watches from a distance closing her eyes in prayer as he staggers back to his feet.

In most great stories, the antagonist reflects the giant nemesis inside the hero that resists the choices that will define him as hero. In *Rocky*, the real antagonist is the main character's self-doubt and complacency, the threat of ultimate corruption. Rocky Balboa, in his own words, has "lost his confidence." He is on a downward spiral toward mob thuggery; yet, his conscience still speaks within him so there is a glimmer of hope. Rocky wants better and is a preacher in his own way on the streets of South Philly that things can be better, though his companions in the same misery reject him. The projected giant who represents the exaggerated antithesis of Rocky's failed life is Apollo Creed, current heavyweight champion of the year, a boasting Goliath of the ring and current darling of the financial machinery controlling the ring. The climax of the story comes when Rocky fights Creed, not to displace him as the boastful warrior, but to exorcise him as the tormenter of his own soul. When Rocky goes "the distance" with the champion, he recovers his dignity and is made fully human once again.

Then there is the character of Adrian, a loser like Rocky, working in the claustrophobic clutter of a pet store where she tends the counter and cleans cages. The store, like Rocky's apartment, seems the last stop before her life slides into an empty place of impotence and misery. As matters unfold she goes from Cinderella in servitude to redeemed beauty, sleek and decked in a red beret standing in support of her champion like Iris in *The Natural*. Adrian questions Rocky on their first date about his boxing, as it is part of a world so far from her own. Yet, the love that develops between the two is of heaven. He helps her around an ice rink, protects her from her drunken brother, restores her dignity, and honors her after the great fight. As reporters ply Rocky with questions about a rematch with Creed and how he feels, he searches the crowd and calls her name. "I love you" is all they can repeat to each other once rejoined, and in this moment this unlikely film brings us to tears. Their love is of the heavenly kind and that love makes them not just significant, but holy. She is now the archetypal, pure woman who inspires the hero and exists within his love and affirmation. He, the hero, now serves and honors the woman and lives within her grace and beauty. All around in the crowd are the people redeemed by vicarious participation in the sacrificial victory they have seen and as witnesses to the sublime intimacy that has made it all possible. A miracle has occurred, a transformation of common elements to divine. One of the greatest exhibitions of boxing stamina ever witnessed, the announcer says. The camera dissolves the redeemed community into the background in these final moments as Rocky and Adrian embrace, their love essential, the rest accidental.

One of the films studied by director John Avildsen prior to shooting *Rocky* was the 1954 classic *On the Waterfront.* Rocky's words spoken to Adrian prior to the fight that if he goes the distance with Creed he will become someone echoes Terry Malloy telling his brother Charlie in the famous cab scene that if he had been allowed to beat Wilson he would not be the mob bum he has become. In the climax of *On the Waterfront,* Terry wins over the dock workers by courageously getting up from the ground and walking them to the dock after a severe beating from the mob boss and his thugs. *Rocky* likewise shares visual qualities with the great Elia Kazan film and its gray and hazy environment where lonely union workers try to make a buck and survive the corruption all around them against the backdrop of a seemingly indifferent universe. The role of Adrian reflects Edie Doyle, the heroine of the Kazan film, the blonde innocent who falls in love with Terry and inspires him to break free from the hellish forces pulling him downward to final damnation. In one memorable scene in *On the Waterfront,* Terry walks Edie toward her home and stops beside a fence to speak with her about his life. In *Rocky* a similar scene against a fence depicts Rocky's vulnerability as the local boss Gonzo reprimands him for not breaking a worker's thumb for failure to pay a debt. The only observers of Rocky's caged misery seem to be the power poles and lines that stretch across the sky, the overall shape suggesting crosses hanging over the city. The difference in the two scenes hinges on the presence of the woman. In *On the Waterfront,* Edie is with Terry and is sympathetically listening. In Avildsen's film, Adrian has not yet entered the action to redeem, so we are left with little hope beyond Rock's general likeability.

The journey Rocky undergoes is a kind of passion play, though he physically survives in the end, barely. His character seems born to suffer for the sins of many, traveling through a wasteland under the dark rule of the mob, striving to persevere against impossible obstacles, sacrificing his own good for the sake of the poor and oppressed. And behind it all is the smiling providence in the words of the old hymn. The icon of Christ over the ring in the initial scene functions like the smiling Jesus on the crucifix of the minister's church in *Babette's Feast.* It signals a kind providence allowing this extreme suffering to bring good to others.

To appreciate these elements in the film, it is necessary to see Rocky as the champion of the lost land of South Philly portrayed in the early scenes. When he walks to his dumpy apartment at the beginning of the action, he passes a gathering of local musicians counting out their bits of time around a burning trash can. Later, he pulls a young neighborhood girl from that crowd and walks her home. His lecture to her on reputation, having a "bad rep," is designed to encourage her to break free, the very thing Rocky desires, but she dismisses him with an obscene gesture for his trouble. Here are the lost souls doomed by the dehumanizing and anonymous urban malaise. When Rocky steps into the ring to fight Creed, these are the faces interspersed in the crowd, analogous to those shouting for blood in the first scene, but here awake to the hope that he might show them a way out of that base existence. One of the great virtues of the film is that these deeper associations are subtle. We have no Jimmy the Batboy character who overtly represents the crowd.

We do have the character of Paulie, however, drunken brother of Adrian who fears his life will be limited to the walled hell of the meat locker where he works. Paulie's character pulls together many of the plot elements. He abuses Adrian by confining her to his small row house and berating her, largely because he needs her company and domestic services. Yet, he is sympathetic even so. When he calls Adrian a lost, "busted" woman because of her relationship with Rocky, the hero refrains from breaking Paulie's jaw when Paulie pathetically whimpers, "I can't haul meat no more." His abuse of his sister is just an extension of the curse fallen upon the whole land. Rocky recognizes this, as he has just himself escaped a further plunge into the leg-breaking domain of the devil, the role of pawn to the local mob boss; Gazzo's assistant has been insistently, demon-like baiting Rocky by calling him a "bum." To fix Paulie, Rocky will need to die for him. Ironically, even that local mob boss, Tony Gazzo, comes across as a sympathetic soul. He offers Rocky money to date Adrian and to train for the fight, and then he eagerly watches the battle alongside the other South Philly denizens. He, too, likely fell into this world, a Terry Malloy character never offered an Edie to pull him out.

The criminals in Rocky all have a conscience and the ability to will the good. The trainer Mick offers to work with Rocky partly for self-interest, his chance at a significant role in a real fight, but also for the sake of humanity. He acknowledges his life a waste and wants a way back. "I'm seventy-six years old," he says through the bathroom door as Rocky relieves himself; he knows he deserves nothing. Rocky accepts his offer to manage out of mutual sympathy and desperation. In a way they court each other, their paths both scarred by compromise and bad fortune. When Mick finishes his argument for how he can help, Rocky shouts after him that his house stinks and he will get his face kicked in by Creed, but Rocky still chases Mick down in the street and agrees to the offer. One must finally decide something. Adrian does as well. After being humiliated by Paulie who forces her to go out with Rocky on Thanksgiving, she chooses to prepare herself, straightening her glasses in the mirror. She will go and try to be pretty, she decides.

People must exercise their will to escape; otherwise the apocalyptic earth swallows them whole. Left to the trajectory of seeming fate, Rocky will become the leg-breaker. Paulie will succumb to drunkenness and gives himself over as useful stooge to Gazzo. The young girl will become a whore. Mick will die in obscurity. Adrian will dry up.

Rocky is the fallen crusader knight. He represents all those who have the potential to achieve but are lost in the mists of obscurity. He really does have talent, just as Adrian behind the glasses does hide a beauty that will come out in the end.

The character who moves in the opposite direction in the film, at least in this original of the series and not the sequels, is Apollo Creed. He is a man with brains but a captured soul. When he comes out for the final fight, he sits atop an Uncle Sam float calling out in mockery, "I want you!" It might be what the devil would say to the lost souls of South Philly. Still behind the bluster, the early scenes of the film show Creed a shrewd businessman and promoter. His challenger has gotten hurt. He needs a replacement, a novelty, a local, "the Italian Stallion." He picks Rocky because the name is so easy to mock, and mock him he does; he counts his winnings before the feat is accomplished, one might say. Meanwhile, his manager is watching Rocky more carefully. Rocky is lefthanded which is a problem to many fighters used to righthanded opponents, and Rocky displays a strange ferocity which the promoter notes as Rocky in shown in a local news cast beating carcasses of beef in the locker where Paulie works.

Creed represents American urban corruption, the dynamic implicit in the film as the great antagonistic force, business taken to the level where conscience plays no part. He is like the local who becomes the scout and spy for the enemy because he knows so well the territory that the barbarians want to overrun. Creed loves money and notoriety most of all and has embraced America as the place where both can be made. His boxing talent, which Rocky acknowledges over and again—he's the best—has been made subservient to his materialist dream. In that position, he is a different shape to a cloud of Mordor hanging over the land Rocky and Adrian and Paulie inhabit. All the while Rocky's story is unfolding in a redemptive direction, Creed remains unmoved and dull. Only in the end as the two hang on to one another at the end of Round 15 does his humanity sneak through, "Ain't gonna be no rematch," spoken in the slang of his real self, the self still alive under the posing.

As suggested earlier, many critics have hesitated to acknowledge the importance of the film. It is too working-class American; Sylvester Stallone is not to be considered a serious actor; nor is director John Avildsen to be taken seriously. The low budget of the production seeps through in moments. The ending is too happy, and especially with the freeze-frame of Rocky and Adrian in their embrace. Still, *Rocky* has had a strangely long shelf life, with a newness each time it is viewed.

Dorothy Sayers speaks of the "rightness" of great art in a way that might explain the anomaly:

> *Our perfect writer is in the act of composing a work—let us call it the perfect poem. At a particular point in this creative act he selects the "right" word for a particular place in the poem. There is only one word that is "dead right" in that place for the perfect expression of the Idea. The very act of choosing that one "right" word, automatically and necessarily makes every other word in the dictionary a "wrong" word. The "wrongness" is not inherent in the words themselves—each of them may be a "right" word in another place…*[13]

Sayers' point is drawn from her Trinitarian approach to the creative process. The artist begins in the realm of the Father with a guiding Idea, then executes that Idea in the realm of the Son, and that execution, the art which emerges, carries strange influence over those who read or watch or listen in the domain of the Spirit who controls artistic influence in the service of the Father and Son—that is, the Idea and its execution. Her assessment of the mysterious, "right" word comes from her examination of the process of execution, the realm of the Son. The "right" word is a living thing, just as all of us with our personal strengths and weaknesses, our idiosyncrasies, bear a uniqueness that suggests craft. We have been crafted from a common mold in a unique way. All our parts contain an inherent rightness, something objective and not merely a matter of perception.

*Rocky* works because all the unique details seem exactly right for the conception. Consider Stallone's characterization of the hero. It is perfectly authentic, less a performance than something that came out of the man naturally. His character, its rightness and believability, drives the film. It appears in the way he moves, the way he plays with a handball while walking along, the way he speaks. It is part of his whole expression. "Yo, Adrian" has become a cultural cliché, a symbol of the success of the franchise; yet, it comes across in the original as completely natural and authentic to the character and setting. Likewise, the costuming of Rocky and Paulie and the early, mousy Adrian seem exactly right. The Philadelphia street scenes in the neighborhood seem a perfect realization in small form of that little spot of geography in that particular spot of 1970's time. Gazzo driving alongside Rocky in his clumsily large sedan and with his abusive assistant works perfectly, as the moment does when Rocky tries to reach into the car to get at the belligerent assistant. This rightness is not easily explained either, any more than one might explain the rightness of the shape of a particular tree or a great painting. It is something perceived, the thing that makes a work of art last over time and evoke a universal response.

Take the scene when Rocky brings Adrian to his apartment. She hides in her coat and hat, face half hidden behind plain glasses. Meanwhile he removes his sweater revealing his impressive build in what the kids in my neighborhood called a dago-T. How that scene unfolds is key to the entire film. Is their meeting appropriate? Is she safe? Rocky reaches into a fishbowl and lifts out two turtles. "These are the exotic animals I was telling you about. These are my friends, Cuff and Link." Her hesitancy and his authentically nervous attempts at wooing make the scene plausible to anyone who recalls truthfully their awkward first steps into courtship. Rather than come directly to the couch where he has planted himself, she takes a sharp turn to the mirror to look at his few family pictures. "Are these your parents? Is this you?" When she expresses worry that her brother Paulie does not know where he is, he opens the window and yells out, "Yo, Paulie. Your sister is with me. I'll call you back later." The entire scene unfolds with a simple charm and then to a hesitant first kiss that seems somehow "right."

This is not to suggest, of course, that the film cannot be criticized. The music, for example, especially in the sequence when Rocky trains in preparation for the culminating fight, does date to the 70s and its love affair with the synthesizer. The fight sequences in the ring are indeed exaggerated, though not all that different perhaps than a battle sequence in an Arthurian tale or a scene out of Homer. Creed comes across a touch too much a caricature in places, at least against the authenticity of Stallone's performance; yet, the same criticisms might be and have been levied against many classics of the past, like Griffith's *Broken Blossoms* (1919) or any number of period films. Rocky might not stand up well against the film that influenced it, *On the Waterfront*, but that is comparing an exceptional little film to a world masterpiece, and so rather unfair. The flaws in *Rocky* largely result from budget limitations, not from a lack of authentic creative energy. Given those limitations, despite those limitations, it completely works; that is the point.

At the time of this writing, the Rocky franchise has grossed nearly 1.7 billion dollars, and this all beginning with a film boasting a miniscule one-million-dollar budget. Such a financial return cannot be attributed to good marketing or production savvy. It speaks to the nerve the film touched. In 1976, America's bicentennial year, the general populace was not faring well. The inflation rate in 1975 was 9.13%. Unemployment was at 9% in 1975 and 8% in 1976. America was only three years removed from the disastrous Vietnam War, one year from when the conflict officially ended. The previous year's Academy Award winner for Best Picture was the dark comedy, *One Flew Over the Cuckoo's Nest*, in which the hero rebel earns a lobotomy for his troubles. Like Rocky Balboa, the country seemed to be in severe decline; thus, the soil was right for its Cinderella message.

The success of the film depends on its smallness of focus. The Philadelphia depicted in the film is hardly a bustling metropolis. There are no extras filling the streets where Rocky walks—this is where the low budget proved a happy accident. The mood that dominates the action is loneliness. Rocky is a solitary character. He lives in a cramped apartment on a quiet and depressed street of row houses. He visits Adrian in a local pet store which seems to have few customers. On their first date, he walks her around an empty ice-rink, observed only by the manager who is eager that they finish so he can go home. He pounds meat with only Paulie to watch. He trains in the early morning when few are awake. It is not until the end when in the arena that the world seems larger than the few streets he haunts, and that scene is introduced by one when he enters the arena alone at night and notices the promotional poster has the colors on his trunks wrong. The film's smallness of focus captured a significant gestalt in the American experience. On the deeper level, Rocky is the small and lonely saint who fasts and prays when the world sleeps, and who sacrifices himself as those martyrs whose blood was the seed of the Church. This combination of cultural marker and archetype explains why the film has touched so many in the years since its release. The country was full of lonely men who saw little ahead of them but a longshot lottery ticket. And perhaps, this is the common state of man.

A most moving scene is that one when Mick comes to visit Rocky in his apartment to offer his services as trainer. Life has passed Mick by, and so he presents an emblem of what Rocky could become. As he describes his past successes and troubles in the ring, courting Rocky like a desperate lover, Rocky grows more and more agitated. He retreats to the bathroom leaving Mick to continue his appeal through the door. The toilet flushes. Mick finally gives up and retreats, and Rocky begins to crack. "What about me, Mick," he shouts. Look where he is living. The place "stinks," he shouts, banging his forearm on the door. Finally, his frustration spent, he hurries down to the street where he catches up with Mick and makes peace. It is a beautiful scene of two desperate men finding strength to join forces to choose a way out and up.

When Stallone received his Academy Award, he dedicated it to all the Rockys out there. The modern world has produced many Rocky types, men with lost dreams buried in some crowd heading who knows where. The pounding Rocky takes in the ring is metaphoric. Hit me again. "Cut me, Mick." Rocky embraces his Passion because it is about self-respect and fraternity. He needed the chance to announce himself that he is not just an anonymous bum.

A good cross-reference for this aspect of *Rocky* is the a1956 sleeper film *Marty* starring Ernest Borgnine. That film tapped a similar nerve en route to its four Academy Awards. An overweight butcher falls for a plain local girl but is harassed by his friends and mother into nearly abandoning her and so giving up on life. At the end, he realizes his folly,

> *You don't like her, my mother don't like her, she's a dog and I'm a fat, ugly man! Well, all I know is I had a good time last night! I'm gonna have a good time tonight! If we have enough good times together, I'm gonna get down on my knees and I'm gonna beg that girl to marry me! If we make a party on New Year's, I got a date for that party. You don't like her? That's too bad!*

Marty calls Clara at the end and affirms his life, and the audiences responded, both in the States and overseas. Something about the deadening anonymity produced by the modern world seemed exorcised by the film. One must step forward and live. A man must act.

In the end Rocky chooses to fight. What drives him, as in the first scene with the club fighter, is anger, but of a good kind. When Creed starts to knock him around the ring and calls him a "Chump," he loses his temper, and that temper compels him to say no to the angel of death. Come on, he gestures to Creed after a scuffle in the corner. He will die in the ring if needed, and with the joy of a martyr.

The same might be said of Adrian, who lives her own Cinderella captive existence serving her abusive brother Paulie. "I've been good to you, Paulie," she screams in exasperation. "I take care of you." Paulie in his own misery has played her affections and made her into what he himself is becoming, a nobody addicted to self-defeating habits. When Rocky tries to coax Adrian into staying with him in his apartment that first night, she makes up excuses, testing to see if he just wants to own her as Paulie does; yet, the audience knows better of her champion. What she desires is what he finally provides, that her knight would acknowledge before God and men that to live and to love and to serve faithfully another small soul is the highest calling in life, however implausible such a vocation may seem to the defeated denizens of the cold daylight. She wants to be loved, and like the Velveteen Rabbit in another poignant story, once Rocky loves her, she is made real.

# 7
# TO KILL A MOCKINGBIRD

*Take God for your spouse and friend and walk with him continually, and you will not sin and will learn to love, and the things you must do will work out prosperously for you.*

—St. John of the Cross

At the start of this book, we set out to highlight the inner awakening that aesthetic beauty, and specifically cinematic beauty, sparks. Our interest was less on ideas formed in the mind than on longings aroused in the heart. We asserted that the cinematic art which moves us most deeply taps most deeply into the spiritual tendencies that define us as human. *We long for love, and we long for heaven, for we sense we are made for both. We weep in those tender moments of a film because we have lost hold of elements of our own time.*

Few films prove these assertions so well as Robert Mulligan's masterpiece *To Kill a Mockingbird* (1962). We are deeply moved in the same places. "Miss Jean Louise? Miss Jean Louise, stand up. Your father's passin'." That's the first. Then later when Sheriff Tate asks Scout whom she saw carrying Jem, and she says, "There he is Mr. Tate. He can tell you his name." And behind the bedroom door, standing, shrinking, Boo Radley appears, luminous and innocent. Then, in the voiceover with an older Jean Louise closing the storybook with a poetic flourish, interpreting the contents for us, the camera discretely staying outside the bedroom window as the younger Scout, fresh from the miracle of walking Boo Radley home, buries her head in the chest of her father, "I was to think of these days many times of Jem and Dill and Boo Radley and Tom Robinson… and Atticus. He would be in Jem's room all night. And he would be there when Jem waked up in the morning."

All three moments present to us displays of tender goodness and spark a profound longing, one rarely evoked in this life beyond our most treasured personal memories. It is the longing for a time when our pride might swell with the privilege of participation in a virtuous heroism. It is the longing for another token of the love of our own shy fathers who hide in plain sight behind some half-closed door. It is the longing for a heavenly mother to hold us, to ensure we sleep peacefully through the night. Bundled together these remind us as well of those few fleeting moments in the past when we felt we were loved, truly loved.

It is said that nothing affects the psychological development of a child so adversely as the loss of a parent, be it through death or divorce or abject betrayal or worse. That horror is the reality behind the real Freudian repression—not that our fathers have violated a taboo and let out some monster, but that our fathers may disappear from our lives, plain and simple. We push that fear far back into the corner of our consciousness and shut down the room lights to cloak it from our vision, for it challenges what we most desire to be true—that we have been held at the heart without question and will be held without end. The child wants to be secure and proud of his or her father, to bring him out into the open for all to see and admire, but what if when the curtain opens, he is gone?

Atticus Finch is the center of *To Kill a Mockingbird*, and not because he defends the black man, Tom Robinson, nor because he was so perfectly realized in the Academy-Award performance of Gregory Peck. He is the center because he is an emblem of the father, real or imagined, that we all secretly cherish. He is the sweetest-singing mockingbird in a story about mockingbirds. His integrity and his steadfastness prove him worthy of the hopes of his children, and worthy of the golden memories that drove Harper Lee to conjure him into being. To question one's father in life or memory is so tempting to do, but so risky. We need to take more care. What if the misunderstood man in our world meant only to love in the one way he knew how? Atticus Fitch confirms for us that heroic fathers can and do exist, though rare. He gives us hope, and that hope spurs us to reach out once again to the flawed man who stands in our shadows. It renews our idea that another Father waits for us beyond the clouds.

The story of *To Kill a Mockingbird* as in life presents many false fathers, and only a few who are true. Bob Ewell, the prime antagonist, beats his daughter Mayella Ewell for kissing a black man, Tom, and then bullies her into blaming the innocent one for her injuries to satisfy his wounded vanity and class envy. He curses and spits upon Atticus, and later assaults Atticus' children, because that good man is his antithesis and so his accuser. It's Luciferian behavior really. But Bob Ewell is only one of many false fathers. His image is reflected on the leering face of the court prosecutor and the blank-faced jurists who side with Bob Ewell to condemn Tom. It's also on the faces of the men from Old Sarum who confront Atticus at the jail with the intent of conducting a lynching. When one of the mob grabs Jem hard to pull him out of the way of their devious intention, we get a foreshadowing of how Bob Ewell will break Jem's arm later—"He's got a bad break, so far as I can tell. Somebody tried to wring his arm off," says Dr. Reynolds. And there are still others, like Dill's absent father. Dill tells Jem and Scout he doesn't have a father when they first meet and then later lies, we assume, about his father's wealth and noble intention to set Dill up in real style later. And there is Boo Radley's father, Nathan, who cements the entrance to the cradle in the tree where Boo leaves Jem his treasures. And Walter Cunningham's father, a poor man who can barely provide meat for his children and should know better, but who shows up with the Old Sarum mob to transfer his own shame onto the scapegoat Tom.

As for the true fathers in the story, foils for Atticus, two stand out—Tom himself and Boo Radley. Unfortunately, neither is allowed opportunity to carry through their desires to love and fully protect their children. Tom, a good, honest man, as Atticus proclaims in his defense, runs like a crazy person to his death, leaving behind his wife Helen and their house full. The last image of the narrative surrounding the trial shows Tom's suffering wife Helen collapsing on the porch when Atticus brings news of the poor man's death. As for Boo, tender and watchful as a good father must be, he has been imprisoned by his small-minded father Nathan, a smaller version of Bob Ewell, except for that golden while when he is able to leave a few gifts, and later given the grace and opportunity to save the children: "Thank you, Arthur, for my children," Atticus says, shaking his hand. But Boo is simple and captured and thus incapable of fully exercising his kindly will.

Atticus is on display as the paternal emblem from the opening moments of the story when the children run to meet him on his return journey from the courthouse, when Jem takes his briefcase and Scout hangs on his arm. On the way home, he tames old Mrs. Dubose, a morphine addict in the Harper Lee novel. We watch him defer wisely to Walter Cunningham's father who cannot catch up on his legal bill. Later we see him shoot a mad dog. "Didn't you know your daddy is the best shot in the county?" Heck Tate tells the astonished Jem. These smaller revelations prepare for his defense of Tom Robinson—an "unpleasant business" as Maudie Atkinson will tell the children later, the kind of business allotted to the divinely appointed, strong very few.

Like any father, Atticus must be tested and by his children. The action of the story is recounted principally through their studying eyes, most literally in the attack scene in which Scout peers without full comprehension through the eye-slit of her costume for the Halloween pageant. The children act as witnesses to his own trial, and by the end he is proven authentic and so etched permanently in the loving tableau. This explains why the three scenes recalled at the start of this chapter have such power.

In the first, the jury has given their evil verdict against Tom, and the courtroom disperses with even the judge slamming his door in disgust at the injustice allowed. Atticus is left alone to pack his briefcase and consider the appeal he intends to file, except that in the gallery the black folk supporting Tom remain. A few of the women rise first, and then all rise as Atticus begins his walk down the aisle and out. Scout, without full comprehension, remains on the ground at the minister's feet. That's when Reverend Sykes, a look of profound respect on his bespectacled face, utters his admonition for her to also rise. That reverend Sykes refers to Atticus as "passin" carries special resonance, as the "passin" most colored people knew best was with those trying to gain respectability by playing white. Here, Atticus has taken on the shoes of the poor black folk that he represents.

In the second, Boo Radley emerges from behind the bedroom door; yet, not as the imagined "spook," but as another child. Atticus steps over to the door to introduce to Scout "*Mr.* Arthur Radley." As Atticus knows Boo and has apparently shielded him all along, this moment has tremendous power for Scout and for those secretly watching. It is the reveal of the great mystery that captivated the children in their various games around the Radley house—touching the door, peering in the window. And that the greatest perceived horror would be revealed as the source of the purest love, the hidden friend, how beautiful. Boo is imaged as lightness and simplicity in that scene and the one to follow. His hair is strikingly blonde. His movements are awkward but tender. "You can pet him if you want," Scout urges Boo who stands tremulous over Jem's bed.

The last revelation is the final of the film, and the sweetest. It is the closing image of Atticus waiting beside Jem's bed—so tender that the camera will track back discreetly to keep all the children sleeping gently on their bed of time. The scene was foreshadowed earlier when Atticus read to Scout on her bed. Reading is her favorite ritual with Atticus, we discover. She won't let him go so easily when the book closes, and she asks to see his watch—notably, Boo will leave Jem a watch in the tree cradle, and that watch will figure prominently in the box of treasures Jem will show Scout, treasures first revealed in the film's opening credit sequence. Will she get the watch? No, it is "customary" for the watch to pass from father to son. She will get a ring and pearl necklace that belonged to her mother. And what she does not yet know, she will receive the treasure of appointment as narrator for the story to be told. And so, she will be privileged to paint that final portrait of father and child.

The lost mother must also be remembered. The bedtime reading scene with Scout folds into Atticus on the porch hearing Scout and Jem in their beds, Scout asking about her mother, Atticus' wife. Scout can't recall her as she was only two years old at her death. Was she pretty, Scout asks Jem, the natural question from a child who wants to hold tight such a memory. Yes, she was. Atticus hears the exchange and ponders it silently, sorrowfully we understand. He holds his pain inside. He is the loving father without a wife to help him through the toughest of times, though Maudie Atkinson functions as surrogate in a few scenes—explaining how good a lawyer Atticus is when Jem feels betrayed by Atticus' refusal to play football, joining Atticus at the breakfast table when Scout is off in a dress for her first day at school, then in the scene when Atticus learns of Tom's death. "We had more than a good chance" of winning the appeal, Atticus says in his frustration and grief. Maudie stays silent, respectful of the accumulation of the good man's grief. The dead wife and mother, not Boo Radley, is the secret in the hero's life.

These three powerful scenes—the courtroom passin', Boo's emergence, and the quiet benediction at the end—are all cued by the bittersweet Elmer Bernstein film score. The music that weaves so well the elements of the story together is one of the film's most memorable features. In the opening credit sequence, all we hear at first is Scout's humming as she colors over the letters of the title and draws other simple images. Then the music begins in full orchestration triggering the emotional river the events will course upon. It perfectly captures the mood of the story of memory and childish simplicity. These are legacies of a time never to be captured again—significantly, by 1962 when the film was in production, Maycomb County had so modernized that Universal decided it would be easiest to rebuild the town of Maycomb, Alabama, on a back lot.

The action begins on the tail end of the Depression, which had hit the farmers worst, Atticus tells Scout, though they were all poor. The street supported few cars and no concrete. The children played free without shoes until 10pm when Atticus would start to worry about their whereabouts.

When I was a boy growing up in Chicago in the early to mid-1960s, we still played on the street all afternoon after school until the sun disappeared into the grey horizon beyond the apartment buildings on Ridgeway Avenue, and we lived, it seemed, just a few steps away from the magical, parallel world of the Little Rascals with high drama was played out every day between the buildings. Our block had its own Mrs. Dubose. Mrs. M., our neighbor widow, who would get so upset with us when a tennis ball flew over the roof of our corner bungalow onto her small strip of lawn between the properties. "Why do you boys keep throwing the ball over the roof," she would say, every time, standing on her lawn in bathrobe and gold slippers. We had our familiar stores on Lawrence Avenue and knew all the storekeepers who huddled around their shops in the late afternoon sharing the latest and keeping an eye on us boys. "Fraser, your father. He is a good man, your father. Nicest man." That's what the tailor would say when I came in with a pair of my father's baggy trousers. I would reply with a shy smile as Scout or Jem might. My brother and I walked the mile and a half home from school every day and dawdled all the way. There were a couple of mean men here and there. One kept his son cooped up amidst stacks of newspapers filling his dirty, run-down place. And there was the Crazy Man who worked at the corner convenience store, though we never called it that, just the Store. The poor man had a palsied hand, and we invented all sorts of terrible stories why. And school yard or street corner fights were also part of our neighborhood ritual. No girls involved, though a few tomboys played sports with us. I once split the lip of a girl playing goalie with a high shot, and she cried like a girl. That ended that.

But the world was already a different place, as a major change was occurring, one that would become most evident with the assassination of John F. Kennedy in 1963 and then Vatican II. Everyone felt the tide shifting, and so we had begun to experience that gnawing nostalgia for something better but lost. On the television set, there was old Andy Griffith of Mayberry. On film there was… "Maycomb was a tired old town – even in 1932 when I first knew it – that summer I was six years old." Already by 1962 when the film was produced, such a slower age meant once upon a time, a psychological reality that directs us now to a key technical detail of Mulligan's master work, the choice to film in black and white. When Martin Scorsese made a similar choice in 1980 for his *Raging Bull* to capture the grittiness of the boxing world and the mindset of his main character, critics saw it as genius. In *To Kill a Mockingbird* the choice seemed and seems more inevitable. On one thematic level, the film is about black and white. On a broader level, it is about moral clarity, the respect for black and white. The main reason for the choice is texture. This film had to be black and white like an old photo from a bygone era attached to an article from *Reminisce* magazine.

That sense of nostalgia is part of the film's mystique, and perhaps the principal reason for its universality. Almost everyone we knew from our era and before could repopulate the story with characters from their own. What we couldn't often do was replicate the film's moral clarity. That's another reason why *To Kill a Mockingbird* moves us so. Advocates of the social revolution spreading up in the late sixties would make the story a racial anthem. The marketers and educators who promoted the book and film played their part as well. Civil Rights were coming more and more into public view. Yet, very few people around us saw the film as a story of racial tensions and reconciliation. Those matters of relationship were the stuff of our common life. We lived in the cultural melting pot of Chicago and worked out our differences in the old fashion—and there were many differences that involved race, class, and religion. For us *To Kill a Mockingbird* was not about those issues but rather about rising above human tragedy through beauty and integrity and loyalty, and all centered in the character of the father, Atticus, the wonderful father whom we respected though few of us knew as a reality.

This all suggests an underdiscussed aspect of the film, which is the final confrontation between Heck Tate and Atticus while on the porch after the assault and the revelation of Boo's protective love. Our hero has a flaw, we discover. Atticus trusted the law of man perhaps more than the law of God. He says as much at the trial—the court of law in America is where all men and women are levelled, where justice can triumph. Well, not really. His lament that they had such a good chance at the appeal comes across as a bit naïve. Tom Robinson had no chance. In the final scene with Heck and Atticus, the father first suggests that Jem had killed Bob Ewell. "You think your son killed Bob Ewell, Mr. Finch…." As the conversation progresses, Atticus suggests a trial for Boo Radley. Heck turns on the thought. To take Boo into the limelight, the man who brought the town and Atticus justice, would be a sin. And that sin he does not want on his head. "I may not be much, Mr. Finch, but I'm still sheriff of Maycomb County, and Bob Ewell fell on his knife. Good night, sir." Scout joins in afterward as the kindly angel, "It would be sort of like shooting a mockingbird, wouldn't it?" This is a crucial moment as Atticus' weakness is exposed before Heck, Scout, and the audience. His back is turned from the camera as Heck admonishes him. "Bob Ewell fell on his knife, Mr. Finch." Class was an issue for Atticus, who was a bit too much the Southern gentleman; he was a man like all men who needs a dose of frank truth from time to time. Heck provides it in the moment. Scout will provide it in the benediction of her story.

Atticus' belief in civil law ties to his silence on the matter of his wife's death. There is a time to rail like David or Abraham, as, finally, God is the arbiter of justice and the only one who can right the balance. Reverend Sykes represents the unspoken truth, his community being one that cannot afford the naivete Atticus teases. Bob Ewell spits in Atticus' face and attacks his children, and that villain ends up with a kitchen knife stuck up under his ribs. Helen Robinson and the community around her have only the mercy of God to rest upon, and the promise of a final judgment and their faith. Tom is gone forever.

This weakness in Atticus comes out in the trial as well, as much of his assault on the testimony of Bob and Mayella Ewell hints at their ignorance and baseness. He has "nothing but pity for them." He is allowed to say that being a white man, while Tom is finally confirmed to be guilty by inadvertently admitting that he "felt sorry" for Mayella. Tom's sentiment violates a taboo for a black man. So, though he does not see it himself, Atticus is as much a product of his environment as the others, though his character is better. When Heck reprimands him, it is with measured heat, and it seems to hit home. Natural law precedes and judges civil law. Atticus has forgotten this, and so implicitly has the whole community. He stands first against the abrogation of civil law he witnesses in the mob. Scout stands with the natural law she recognizes in the simple ways of Boo.

This revelation is crucial to understanding the coming of age of both Jem and Scout. They must learn to see their father as worthy by virtue of his integrity and great deeds, but they must also then learn to see him as fully human and in need of love and forgiveness like the rest of us. We can never truly love plaster saints.

The film's power is centered here. We are overcome because those paradoxical qualities of true fatherhood—strength and vulnerability—are so rare in combination. Boo is vulnerable, tender, but not strong. Atticus is strong and needs to be vulnerable. He needed to weep when hearing his children speak so longingly of their dead mother. Having two mother proxies around the home, Maudie and the maid Calpurnia, is not enough. He needed to be less stiff, as they say, and grieve more. In the end, he does, or so it seems.

It is hard to write these words here and not reflect on my own failures as a father, as perhaps it is hard for these words to fall over any of us. It almost seems unfair that fathers are so mercilessly scrutinized by their children. Mothers have this lane covered. Their position and their pain springs from other sources. But fathers must deal with impossibly high expectations and the terrifying, terrible realization that the narratives of the lives of their children, the ones the children themselves will write, will center explicitly or implicitly on them. I hear "It's finally dad's fault" the way D. H. Lawrence heard "We must have more money" in his childhood home. It echoes softly in the background at every one of our family get-togethers. And I have found self-defense a pointless endeavor. Once an old priest rebuked me in the confessional for just this, when I confessed to being too aggressive in defending my point against some small domestic coup. The words had barely gotten out of my mouth in that dark place, that I had failed, had sinned by trying too hard, when his rebuke came, "Well, that was a pointless venture, wasn't it?" Here we are repeating the words years later, so they made their impression.

Once this element of fragile fatherhood is brought in, other elements of the film fall in place. As much as the story details Scout and Jem coming of age, the coming of age addresses Atticus' position. He needed Boo Radley as much as the children did, and indicates as much when he thanks Boo at the end "for his children." Without Boo's intervention on Atticus' behalf, the story would be tragic, but it is not. *To Kill a Mockingbird* is a comedy in the Aristotelian sense. Atticus' fatal flaw does not unleash the fury of the gods. Rather he is visited by a tender mercy. He is as much wrapped in the cloak of heaven's great mother as he wraps Scout and Jem at the end. Atticus is finally restored to his wife because were she there she would likely have told him the very same as Heck did, and she would have likely intervened earlier to protect the children. Boo acts as her proxy as much as Beatrice does for Dante. His mute timidity recalls the broken angel in the Tolstoy story. Now Boo can return home for good.

The story of *To Kill a Mockingbird* strings together several accidents of grace. No doubt Harper Lee built this in the original from her own experience—her father much the standard-bearer as her main character, friends who would later put up the money for her to take enough time off her airline receptionist job to complete the novel, a timeliness to the publication coming as it did just as the nation was to wake up to its racial history. And then there are the accidents of the film production. That Gregory Peck took the role and not others changed the course of film and American history. The child actors, both unknown and taken from the local community, accomplish nearly flawless realizations. Robert Mulligan, a middling director, who would never achieve anything else so great, played a Michael Curtiz part in his handling of all the delicate details. Robert Duvall entered the film as an unknown and became Boo Radley as no one else can be imagined playing. And, not to be overlooked, Elmer Bernstein, the great composer, adds his mastery, as does Horton Foote who wrote the screenplay, one of the best Southern playwrights of his era.

Every so often creative film magic works this way. An author of just one great book, which is the only great book any of us can author—our life story—gets her work taken immediately to screen while still within the cultural pulse, and the entire production crew captures the dream world and its atmosphere without effort. Something of grace got hold of this film as it did the characters in the film. Jem rolls Scout in a tire which just happens to settle at the base of the Radley steps. A mad dog comes to town and threatens the street where Atticus, the best shot in the county, resides.

Boo just happens to be nearby to hear Bob Ewell assault the children. Bard has only one arrow left in his quiver, the black arrow of his ancestors, and just as he takes hold of its shaft the thrush arrives to whisper in his ear the place on Smaug's breast unprotected from his scales and jewels. Divine providence at work.

Both natural law and divine providence are extensions of secret laws of heaven. C. S. Lewis points out at the start of *Mere Christianity* how children when playing will know instinctively when the rules are broken, even though they have never signed on to the rules point by point. Systems of justice are built into the order of creation. Scout knows intuitively that Boo is a mockingbird, the fiddler on the roof of her story. She understands at the end that natural law requires he be preserved from the laws of men. She also understands that Boo has been her special gift, though she may never quite speak it that way. The laws of men lead to the verdict given by the jury at Tom's trial, but Boo is the messenger bringing heaven's verdict, the story's corrective to the inevitability of human injustice and cruelty. Heck, a character on the fringes, recognizes this—Heck may not be much, but he is a Christian in the fundamental sense. So, too, is the judge who appoints Atticus and sets the action in motion, who understands that Atticus is the only real choice for the dirty job, whose response to the tragedy is to dismiss the jury and slam his chamber door.

Interesting that a film with so distinctly a religious tone defines morality in its last moments as a setting aside of man's law. "Why do you smite me?" Jesus asks when before his judges. Human law in our broken world always seems to eventuate in an undermining of the law of God. Javert ever lurks in the shadows in pursuit of Jean Valjean, the criminal guilty of stealing a loaf of bread to feed his family.

No doubt this is why the bittersweet score of Elmer Bernstein fits so well. The comedy of Atticus embraced by Scout and Jem, of Boo restored to all three, of the town set back to balance after a wave of injustice leaps down the street like the rabid dog, that comedy totters on the edge of the grave. Good triumphs; yet, the situation all around is so ultimately hopeless. Helen Robinson will forever lament the loss of her husband. The black community will continue long after the action to answer to "Boy!" The jurors will ever sit smugly in their homes explaining why their verdicts were not only right and necessary, but virtuous if seen correctly. All these evils will continue to haunt the story after its telling. The little flock is thoroughly surrounded—will the angel of grace come again at the next crisis point to rescue this poor remnant?

One imagines that Harper Lee wrote the story to crystalize her nostalgic memories:

> *So thou through windows of thine age shall see*
> *Despite of wrinkles this thy golden time.*

Shakespeare. Life is a slow loss of all we try to hold tightest—youth, beauty, relationships. It is a poignant fact of life that Harper Lee never wrote a follow-up to *To Kill a Mockingbird.* How could she without diminishing the original and the history behind it? Old Jack Nelson, the English teacher who turned me toward a love for books and poetry once said to a class of dull sophomores at a declining Catholic high school in Chicago what we suggested earlier, "Everyone has one great novel to write, and that is their own life." But what he did not say, and we will say here, is that such a story can only be written correctly once. There is tragicomedy for you. It brings to mind the much quoted words of Tolkien from a letter, "Actually I am a Christian and indeed a Roman Catholic, so that I do not expect 'history' to be anything but a 'long defeat'— though it contains (and in legend may contain more clearly and movingly) some samples or glimpses of final victory."[14]

Scout and Jem and Atticus lose the key battle in *To Kill a Mockingbird.* "Tom Robinson is dead." Atticus offers that final statement to Maudie and the children still gathered on the porch the evening after the trial. Nothing can bring him back. Nothing can spare Helen and the extended family their grief. Bob Ewell will also lie dead, but that bit of vengeance will not erase the lies and degradation of Mayella and the other residents in that dark place. The ingrained racism of the town will not be corrected with Tom's death, though viewers of the film may feel steps have been made, wavering steps carrying the gentle smugness that captures Atticus before Heck corrects him.

The comedy resides in the fact that God has in a strange way revealed himself and restored one family, memorialized in Scout's memory, that can now move forward with the trust that a kindly providence does exist and will one day right the balances. That is the truth behind the story's power. We long for love and permanence and find confidence to move forward in those kindly affirmations of grace that come our way, even when packaged with other sorrows. Who will console Boo once Scout leaves him on the porch of his miserable home? Will he be satisfied enough in the memory of having saved Jem to make his remaining long days pass with pleasantness, or will he perhaps feel the twinge of regret that he had not arrived moments earlier to spare Jem the beating from Bob Ewell? Did he hesitate in coming and so arrive just moments late, and will that trouble him? Will he suffer further abuse at the hands of his father for getting so involved in other folks' business?

And more, will Atticus emerge a better man as result of his trial and the reproof of Heck? He will be loved by Scout beyond the pages of the novel, Harper Lee's own father memorialized through his character, but neither character nor real man will be able to read about it. Harper Lee fulfilled her longing to write, but the writing was directed toward those who were to follow. The writing forever sealed the losses of the world she described. Like Boo, notoriety would not prove welcome to her either. Lee would be hounded by her own ambitions and the merciless critics demanding a sequel. How does one write a sequel to their life story, she must have thought? Why would a writer with integrity even try to write the sequel? It would be madness. Far better to join the ranks of Margaret Mitchell and Ralph Ellison and Boris Pasternak who knew enough to save their life by losing it.

We must save our life by losing it. We have that from good authority. White martyrdom is the preferred course when red is not the color of the fetid cultural stream. *To Kill a Mockingbird* urges us to die, to follow old sense and sit down on the porch swing with Scout and Boo and reflect and then be swept away. Look out upon that street which holds so many memories, but which cannot remain as it appeared once upon a time, and sigh with the poet Hopkins:

*It is the blight man was born for,*
*It is Margaret you mourn for.*

# 8
# THE SEARCHERS

*But, no matter how general bad example may be, it can never make evil lawful or justifiable.*

—The Young Seminarian's Manual

In America, at least since the late nineteenth century when mass media began to take hold, two-dimensional thinking has become the political and cultural norm. That tendency slid into the universities after the politically charged 1960s, and by the time I was in graduate school in the 1980s and first encountered in a serious way John Ford's masterpiece *The Searchers* (1956), intellectual conversations had shriveled to the materialist place where that film remained in the curricular discussion solely as a marker in the development of the Western genre and of the technical evolution in film art, particularly the art of film direction. The complexity of the main character, Ethan Edwards, was pitched in the same terms as Shakespeare's protagonists in his "problem plays," like Antonio in *The Merchant of Venice*—and how can you love a film with a vindictive and even racist hero driving the story? That was where things stood then. Now the devolution of the conversation has led further down the funnel to the ledge where the approved critics trip over one another to label the entire film racist and uncover its perceived socio-political flaws. You need search no further than Roger Ebert who tiptoes awkwardly through a pile of virtue signals in his 2001 retrospective of the film, "In *The Searchers* I think Ford was trying, imperfectly, even nervously, to depict racism that justified genocide; the comic relief may be an unconscious attempt to soften the message." So, the logical degeneration of enlightened discourse has brought us to this sad, only lightly veiled, assertion—In his "masterpiece" *The Searchers* Ford advocated genocide and masked it with comedy, and I am here to help you deal with that dark truth . . . .

Having arrived at such a reductive, irrational level in the approved approach to art, art of whatever kind, the critic now has the wonderful luxury of turning off critical thought. Once the label is placed, what more needs be said? The myriad complexities of plot and character can be dismissed, as can the lived reality behind the art. Brilliant compositions, masterful writing, nuanced performances—all become incidental and finally irrelevant matters.

Enough. For the sake of Chestertonian common sense and sanity, we will start this chapter with an older set of assumptions and approach Ford's film through the lens of its enduring popularity and emotional power. The climactic scene when the conflicted hero Ethan recovers the abducted girl, his niece Debbie, and holds her up to the light and then carries her home tenderly, stands as one of the most poignant moments of any American film. It is a marker of redemption and transcendence, and so the scene that moves us most deeply, the glimpse of heaven made possible by the embrace of divine love. So, we will start there holding in mind the question *why* and then work our way back.

The plot of the Ford film is simple enough. A band of Comanches set a booby trap and savage a homestead in the arid, sparsely populated lands of west Texas. The youngest daughter, Debbie, is not killed but carried off to play a role in a form of political, sex slavery. Ethan Edwards, a drifting former Confederate soldier, still fighting the war in his mind, vows to avenge the brutal crimes and recover Debbie. Ethan's nephew, Martin Pawley, joins him in the search for Debbie, as Ethan had rescued Martin years before when his family was massacred by Comanches. The homestead was that of his brother who had married Ethan's sweetheart when he was gone to fight. Martin had been raised by Ethan's brother, Aaron, and wife Martha. Ethan and Martin will search for five years before finding the band of renegades, killing the leader Scar, and bringing Debbie home.

The story follows a simple if protracted revenge structure. The interest of the plot is in the characters and how they deal with the conflicts of life on the fringes and how they develop through the challenges of their past griefs and the present rescue mission. For Ethan it is how his hatred can give way to mercy; for others, how the native savagery can give way to domestic bliss.

At the start, Ethan greets his brother's family and mistakes Debbie for her older sister Lucy. He gives her a medal of his as a token, clearly finding her charming like her mother whom he still loves. This gesture sets up the complex web of relationships at stake. At the end when Ethan will lift the captured Debbie to the light of the sun, he in effect acknowledges her as that same little girl and chooses to restore the family rather than kill her and keep it stored only as a memory. Destroying Debbie and so defeating Scar had been the logical conclusion of the journey in his wounded mind, as she appears to him a ruin, a soiled thing that would forever give the Indians authority over him. In this Ethan and Debbie are alter egos, both pure of heart but scarred by corrupting circumstances beyond their control. Both desire death rather than a ruined life, and both are restored by natural bonds of charity at the end of the struggle. The beginning and concluding shots of the film establish this parallelism, taken from the doorway of a homestead looking out upon the West, typified by the arid landscape not of Texas but of the iconic Monument Valley where so many were filmed. This is an emblem of the inner story of that old life.

The theme of the story is thus the power of love to redeem, true charity against internal desire, the triumph of grace. Ethan will redeem not only Debbie but himself by seeing her as separate from the stains she acquired when in Scar's "household." Scar's name is significant, of course, as it points to the source of these challenges each character faces, all victims or scapegoats of the unpredictable vicissitudes of the harsh frontier.

Another powerful film comes to mind here with a similar theme, Bruce Beresford's *Black Robe* (1991). The base story for that work came from the diary of a Jesuit priest and canonized saint, Noel Chabanel, who was sent from France to evangelize the Algonquin Indians in the Canadian frontier in the mid-seventeenth century. Chabanel's greatest challenge in his mission, per the diary, was not the distance from home or rigors of frontier life; it was his aversion to the Algonquin people the more time he spent in the culture. He found the tribe not only brutal, but bestial particularly in their treatment of women. Still he vowed to stay with them until taken as a martyr and then slowly learned to love them for who they were, against his own natural aversion. That story was written into a novel by the Irish writer Brian Moore and then taken to film. The climax occurs when the protagonist, called Father Laforgue, arrives at a remote Indian camp after a horrific journey and finds plague devastating the tribe. The local chief tells him that many want to kill him because they see him as a demon. This admission with all he has been through leads Laforgue to weep, and the

Chief responds that a demon cannot weep. Is he a man then? Yes. Will he stay and how long? All his life. And, does he love them—the question that has hovered over all the action. Yes, is the answer. Christ is the answer. The final scene has Laforgue baptizing the tribe, a cross blazoning in the sunlight.

That same internal complexity forms the center of *The Searchers*. Ethan hates the Comanche and sees them as less than human. And in his mind he cannot help but hate them given all he has experienced through the years in that wilderness. He even struggles with Martin who has one-eighth Indian blood. Is this racism? Perhaps, but a racism grounded in a desire for vengeance based on harsh experience. Plug into that formula the other party in *any* feud, and the result comes out the same. Ethan's cause is best understood as a logical extension of all the random brutalities of Western expansion, then topped by the Civil War where Ethan fought on the Confederate side. He hates the Comanche because he has witnessed butcheries at their hands, and those butcheries included those whom he treasured most, his brother and Martha, the woman he loved and lost. The Comanche stand for the loss of his dreams, and the hope of the South, his home. In the film Ethan arrives first at Aaron's burned-out homestead and fights Martin to keep him from entering the ruins to see what he himself witnessed when he went inside. Later he will tell Martin that one of the scalps Scar had kept in his tent was of Martin's mother, another woman whom Ethan buried with his own hands.

The hero of the Western is always an outsider, for his code cannot remain in the civilized new land. He works on the edges to make the new, peaceful town possible, a concept best realized in another Ford Western, *The Man Who Shot Liberty Valance* (1962) where the John Wayne character actually wins a duel for a good but inept local lawmaker by shooting from a hidden distance the villain terrorizing a town. He saves the day by stealth and through an act that would be perceived as criminal in the emerging town's civil code. Like Colin Wilson's "Outsider,"[15] his dark tendencies make him the superior man, the man who must ever be drifting from struggle to struggle.

In *The Searchers* the aspect of Ethan's outsider status is grounded in his experience of genuine evil. He has alone cared for the bodies of women who were brutally raped and murdered. He has lost his true love to of all people his own brother. He has been betrayed by the politicians who seemingly represented his homeland and sent him off to fight. Like any veteran returned from a cruel, irrational war, he is unable to assimilate easily.

Those who want to see Ethan's attitudes as morally reprehensible must never have experienced the isolation that comes from a trip through the Dark Wood and then down those ledges of the underworld. How does one pull back to balance after seeing and suffering the experience of terrible injustice? Noteworthy here is that the generation which celebrated the John Wayne character and made the actor the "Most Admired Man in America" was the generation fresh from the atrocities in and surrounding World War II. The new suburbs springing up across America in the 1950s housed many who were battle-scarred. White paint on a picket fence did not mean a reprise of the world of Laura Ingalls Wilder. A character like Ethan, giant on the big screen, was as cathartic to many as were war victim characters like Fred Derry and Homer Parrish in William Wyler's classic from the decade before, *The Best Years of Our Lives* (1946).

The dramatic foil for Ethan, apart from Debbie, is the renegade leader Scar who reveals that he lost two sons to white men and so took many scalps in exchange. He, too, is on a blood quest, a personally motivated, vengeance mission. The difference will be that Scar does not show any depth in his emotions, nor hope for redemption. He merely hates, and he is ambitious, wanting to earn the admiration and loyalty of other parts of his tribe by virtue of his brutality. He shows no hesitation walking his band of renegades into death traps to support his stature as one who will not back down in the face of danger.

So, Ethan is confronted with a conflict that promises no resolution unless he can transcend the hatred feeding it. Impossibly severe as it appears from an objective distance, in an earlier scene that sets up the climax Ethan nearly succumbs to the temptation to kill Debbie, but Martin prevents him. Martin who himself bears the blood that fuels Ethan's passion understands that one does not often get to choose the circumstances that create such internal conflicts. He functions in this understanding as an agent of grace. He saves Ethan from the damnation awaiting him at the end of his mission if, like Scar, he does not step back from the forces driving him. Providence saves in a separate moment, too, when Ethan is nearly arrested by the Reverend and Captain Sam Clayton for shooting three men in the back. The viewer has seen that this shooting was not premeditated but a response to an ambush against him. The rules of not shooting an enemy in the back did not quite apply to the circumstances. Ethan is spared when news arrives that Scar's band is nearby and Clayton needs Ethan to help stave them off. Ethan is thus allowed another chance to receive the grace of love that captures him in the final moment.

This intervention of providence aligns with the deeper principle at work in the story, again natural law versus civil law. Clayton himself underscores the point. Early in the story, we see him in Aaron and Martha's homestead accepting all manner of deference and hospitality as the important man in the room. Then after the massacre he will lead a showy, self-indulgent funeral service that leads Ethan to shout, "Put an amen to it!" Natural law makes apparent that the best course of action in the circumstances is to pursue the renegades while still possible, not to make a show of position and piety. Ethan is the natural man, and Clayton and all the others know it. When told by the posse to stand down, to let the dead bury the dead and move on, Ethan holds a sullen silence. When that posse finds a dead Indian hastily buried, Ethan shoots the dead man in the eyes to prevent his soul from seeing the afterworld as the Indian would believe. When Ethan and Martin come upon a herd of buffaloes later in the quest, Ethan kills the animals to keep them from feeding the hunted. He understands that a different principle of survival governs in the wilderness. The civil laws of men like Clayton cannot take hold until survival is achieved. It is an assertion one finds running throughout all of Ford's best Westerns, not dissimilar to that behind Heck's very American rebuke of Atticus in the conclusion of *To Kill a Mockingbird.*

The conflict within Ethan comes from the fact that he has mingled with natural law the cruel wiliness of the frontier. He obtains information from a trader named Futterman in exchange for some gold coins and understands that Futterman, seeing the gold, will come after him later to rob him the rest. It is Futterman and two lackeys whom Ethan will shoot in the back after they flee their ambush. Futterman had shot Ethan's hat thinking Ethan was asleep in his bed. That behavior is the normal that Ethan has been infected with.

A confirming scene takes place later when Ethan and Martin are provided information about Scar's whereabouts from a Spanish trader. They are invited into the man's home to rest and eat, and Martin is not only offered food, which he needs, but female company which he does not need. When Ethan gets Martin out of there to find Scar, he tosses Martin's drink in the fire, which then kicks up suggesting the drink would have incapacitated Martin and, no doubt, left him easy prey to robbery or worse. Ethan knows how the games are played. He embraces this set of assumptions as a type of common sense and follows that sense relentlessly, just as he followed his initial vow to the Confederate cause and would not stop fighting even after peace was declared.

But the wily "natural law" of the Futtermans and others encountered in the journey is an ape of the real thing, and Ethan is being pulled, therefore, into something false. It lacks the essential components of love and mercy. Futterman's is the other law of the wild, dog eat dog, an eye for an eye, and maybe a second eye into the bargain. True natural law suggests family loyalty above all else; yet Ethan is pushed to sacrifice Debbie to his vengeance. He is tempted by a false rule, the baseness of those who see opportunity for wealth and advancement as prominent above all virtues. Ethan's temptation finds justification for his cruel pursuit of vengeance because he recognizes the hypocrisy of Clayton and the settlers and the professional military. "That'll be the day," he says when asked if he wants to quit by Clayton early in the story. It is his refrain. He is fixed and hard and knowing, but knowing only to the extent of his bitterness.

True natural law is the law of God. As Aquinas described, it is that set of principles built into creation which ought to lead the soul to receive grace. The first principle of natural law per Aquinas in the *Summa* is, "good is to be done and pursued, and evil is to be avoided." Doing good elevates the soul and prepares it for grace. Doing evil corrupts the soul. The faux law that forms the real antagonist of *The Searchers*, obvious in the case of Futterman and other secondary characters, is best realized in the character of Scar, whose presence teases Ethan until the very end.

Vengeance is never a one-to-one proposition as it plays out in real time. In exchange for the death of his son, Scar takes "many" scalps. In exchange for the life of his brother and that family, Ethan is ready to kill many Indians, and he does. Debbie has been the victim all along; yet, Ethan cannot see her as such. That is always the problem; vengeance does not pursue equitable justice. It tacks on expiation for the sorrow and suffering that follows the act. It always ratchets the situation tighter and threatens the very integrity of the thing it serves.

In the Old Testament the people of Israel are given the "eye for an eye" law from Moses to dispense justice publicly in their courts (Deuteronomy 24):

> *And the Lord spoke to Moses, Saying: Bring forth the blasphemer without the camp, and let them that heard him, put their hands upon his head.... Breach for breach, eye for eye, tooth for tooth, shall he restore.... Let there be equal judgment among you, whether he be a stranger, or a native....*

However, equality in practical affairs does not often follow from that one-to-one proposition as evidenced by Christ's teachings in the Sermon on the Mount and his dealings with offenders. In Mosaic Law the thief must restore fourfold what is stolen, not a simple one to one. Recall that Zacchaeus in the Gospels offers tenfold in gratitude for Christ acknowledging him. Such unequal fines allowed the Law to check the people of God from their tendencies toward an excess of vengeance. In other words, given the opportunity avengers of blood will always take more victims than the one allotted by equity. In a similar way, the Law commands that every seven years debts are to be released. Also, in the case of a manslaughter, the perpetrator may flee to a designated city of refuge to find protection from the avenger of blood, the family member in pursuit of natural justice. Grace and mercy is everywhere embedded in the Mosaic Law when applied to transgressors, allowing the break of the evil cycle that leads men toward greater and greater acts of vengeance.

Tempered law, equitable punishment within fixed limits and allowing opportunity for grace, is the true law, what might be called the deeper law of God. It is what ordinary people recognize immediately as prudent and fair given all the varying circumstance around crimes and aberrant behavior. The character who sees this best in *The Searchers* is Martin. When Ethan tells him of the butchery of his mother as an argument for his own bloodthirst, Martin replies, "But that don't change it." Ethan has miscalculated. The fact that the murder is of Martin's mother and that Ethan buried her with his own hands simply proves that Ethan is now motivated by hatred and anger, not justice. Justice is cool. Martin is aware. Ethan is struggling.

All of this is not to suggest that Ethan should be perceived as a villain in the film. Rather, he is a character inviting sympathy and achieving admiration. He is a real man and so relatable. He has lost so much, been betrayed at every turn. The story implies that he has greater experience with the evils and atrocities of the frontier than even what is shown and implied. He sees himself as a realist and that those who give in to illusions are doomed to be robbed or killed. Early in the journey, Ethan and Marty are joined by Brad, the son of the neighboring Nesby family. Brad was in love with Lucy. When Ethan finally tells Brad that Lucy was killed in the initial raid and that he buried her with his hands, Brad loses control and charges into an Indian band without heed. Martin and Ethan stand back and listen to the rifle shots that indicate how that desperate action results. His act is a suicide of passion, but still a suicide. Ethan would not ever give in to such a defeat.

Late in the film, the Spanish trader who shows Ethan and Martin the whereabouts of Scar's band realizes that Ethan may very well kill Debbie and so he returns Ethan's money as "blood money." This is a key moment as it sets up the final resolution when Ethan chooses correctly and embraces Debbie. That trader, though not honest, is at least distant enough from the events to see correctly how the fundamental principles of right and wrong should apply, despite his own personal compromises. It shocks him that Ethan may have lost his clarity of vision.

In this *The Searchers* touches a universal truth we each wrestle against every day. It is hard to love those whom we do not like. It is hard to turn off the valve of passion when outraged. We feel a certain way and make rash judgments. We leave a gathering with friends and family, and our first thoughts lead to comments about those who annoyed us or who committed some indiscretion. And we punish them quietly with words, even slanders, often without allowing any defense.

Ethan has been a victim. The hidden headline in the plot is that Scar butchered Martha, the woman Ethan long loved. Ford tips this off in several places, most notably in an explanatory scene when Martha caresses Ethan's coat as he prepares to leave. Clayton marks this from the background but has the sense to stay silent. Betrayal and loss of love are deep waters.

A foil for this reality plays out on a lighter level in the subplot involving

Martin and his sweetheart Laurie. While Martin is gone five years in pursuit of Debbie, Charlie McCorry courts Laurie. Charlie is a sham version of Martin, for Martin is courageous and moral and simple-hearted, whereas the rival Charlie, though an ex-soldier, comes across as oily and opportunistic. Still Laurie is tempted to choose him in the typical rebound, just because he is Martin's antithesis and so will provide a slap in the face to her long-departed lover. Significant in this parallel scheme is that Laurie first chose Martin. When he returns from the initial exploration prior to the massacre, she runs to greet him and kisses him passionately. He is taken aback, but happy as she is "prettier than he remembered." This is the frontier after all. Later when Martin must fight Charlie at the not-to-happen wedding between Laurie and Charlie, the camera captures Laurie looking on with distinct pleasure. Ford underscores her reaction in much the same way he underscores Clayton remaining silent in the presence of the secret love between Ethan and Martha. As in many other Westerns, the love ritual goes quick. Folks need get down to the business of tending cows and ensuring their harvest. Life is fragile on the frontier and so more uninhibited. Even so, that love commitment is sacred, grounded in medieval chivalric values, those old Christian values that fortified the Western genre. And as in Dante, the woman holds the ultimate power to choose. And so, why did Martha not wait for Ethan's return?

In a Christian comedy, couples who enter the marriage bed need be pure and single-hearted, whether a priest is around or not. Laurie has waited and remained pure, but only because Martin returns just in the nick of time. Martin like Ethan is more resolute. He does face a few temptations on his long trek with Ethan, suggested best when he is given a very plain Indian squaw to wife in a bartering exchange gone bad, comic specifically because we understand the unspoken full situation. The medieval hero must earn the right to see the grail by virtue of his honor. That is his code. He can kill enemies and leave villages full of widows and orphans but if done in honor all is vitiated. Early in the film when Martin kills an Indian when the band of pursuers is ambushed at a river, Martin drops his head into his arm momentarily. There should be grief when a life is taken. Later he has less hesitation, culminating in his killing of Scar in order to rescue Debbie. Martin stays firm in his commitments, moral and romantic. Laurie, on the other hand, is on the edge of giving in. It mirrors the situation with Ethan and Martha. A poor choice from a lack of patience, and both Ethan and Martha suffer a hefty price for it.

Debbie is the foil for Martin. She has been soiled in a fight larger than herself, but she retains her purity of heart, suggested when she initially tests Martin's love, telling him to leave her to her new people. She tells him she prayed to him at first but has since resigned herself to her circumstances. Yet, in the key moment when she is taken from Scar's tent, she embraces Martin with the passion of a sister, her wave of despair washed over by his love. Martin's virtue earns the love of both Laurie and Debbie.

Westerns celebrate romantic love and family ties above all. This is the bedrock of the new land and the government of the people. Leave us alone to carve out our spot and find our way together. It is the principal commandment of the frontier as it has been formed in the American consciousness, at least up until the point when *The Searchers* was made, the mid-fifties.

The silhouette shots in the doorway of the homestead that frame the film make this plain. We Americans are a proud people. The frontier is our great vista, the expanse of the sky, the ruggedness of the terrain. Our great hero has to be the John Wayne character, the iconic frontier man. We are drawn to him more than Martin because he understands on a deeper level all the costs involved. Some of us do well remember how often Wayne was named the most admired man in America during the 1960s. He embodied the tough guy strong enough to forego his own interests to save both family and community. And he had his vulnerabilities, too. No viewer of *The Searchers* in 1956 would have really thought that John Wayne would kill Debbie in the end, but those same viewers understood the conflict and felt it. Ethan just needed a mercy, a few quiet moments to reflect to snap him out of it. He needed to hold the girl up to the bright light of the sun and see in her the little girl she once was and to see in her the wife and mother he lost, Martha. He needed to be reawakened by love.

Many years ago now, a friend told me to trek to the Poconos for a couple days when I was caught in the emotional drama of a failing relationship. Go into the mountains. You will think better then, he said. Go to the Big Blackfoot River, Paul, and fish for a long morning. That will clear your head. We Americans think this way. Give me Texas. Give me some wide-open space and fresh air to breathe; then I'll know how to live right. God will speak to me then. It's our romantic American civil religion as Robert

Bellah once termed it. It's why we are so distressed by oily politicians and oily preachers. They are the antithesis of what it means to be an American. We won't tolerate a Reverend Sam Clayton for long. Put an amen on it, Reverend.

When we are inside the story of a good old-fashioned Western, we feel comfortably at home. When John Wayne fills the screen, it doesn't matter that he is a little stiff and awkward, that his acting is middling, that his films may be uneven. He stands there iconic like dad, the dad we wish for. He towers over us offering protection. "That'll be the day" makes us smile. We know he can beat 'em all, and he will in the end.

As a small boy I walked down Lawrence Avenue one day holding my arm below the shoulder and hoping someone, a woman would be best, might stop me and ask if I was okay. I see it in my mind as though happening. I wanted someone to think me the heroic victim of a gunfight. Roy Rogers got shot. Shane got shot. John Wayne takes an arrow in the penultimate sequence of *The Searchers*—he even wrote out a last will and testament. That is what men do. We get shot but don't fall in a heap. We bandage the wound, write out a will, and plan the next move.

One measure of the resonance of *The Searchers* would be in the way the film school directors have quoted it. George Lucas uses the homestead massacre imagery in the original *Star Wars*. Luke Skywalker climbs a ledge and sees in the clearing his family legacy in flames. Paul Schrader recast the story in his typically sordid terms in *Hard Core*, where a girl is captured by a mob and trafficked on the West Coast, and her father searches to rescue her. More recently, Liam Neeson would get the same role in *Taken* (2008) where a father goes through hell to recover an abducted daughter from traffickers.

However, *The Searchers* is a more honest film than the many that followed. It is not a film trying to show moral sophistication or make a backhanded point or impress by mechanics, but a human story that turned the Western genre toward difficult themes that worked in a country fresh from a war with Germany and Japan, a country where refugees from that carnage had immigrated to our own neighborhoods. Imagine the conflicted feelings a combat veteran might have felt shopping at a small store run by the type of people he was just trying to kill, and who the government propagandized him to believe needed to be killed.

My neighborhood was Jewish. My family was Scottish Catholic. Yet, we found rituals that taught us to get along, often through some challenge to a baseball or football game—with no pads. It was the way we learned to assimilate. Similarly, my grammar school mixed Irish with Italian Catholic. A tough place. Once a Polish boy named Karl showed up as a transfer student in the sixth grade, and we all hated him for breaking into our group, and for having a name we could not pronounce, and for every day pulling from his lunch bag two slices of white bread and a can of frankfurters. We were all thrilled when Frankie N challenged Karl to a fight in Frankie's own back yard. That seemed a fair fight. Frankie invited his friends who gathered in a circle to watch the massacre. But it did not turn out a massacre, as Karl fought hard for himself and his mother who filled his lunch bag each day and the rest of his family and his Polish community relatives who lived in the apartments along Pulaski Road. It was his baptism into our group because we and our families had all passed through a similar fire. Karl and Frankie would become good friends, and Frankie would later consider the priesthood. This was the America of John Wayne and *The Searchers*. It is mostly lost now.

The Max Steiner score for the movie carries the sadness of loss throughout the story, as does the Stan Jones theme song "Ride Away," sung with the perfect pitch of lonely country by the Sons of the Pioneers, "What makes a man to wander? What makes a man to roam? What makes a man leave bed and board and turn his back on home? Ride away…" For those who have never had to ride away to fulfill military duty or to find work out of state or go in search of political sanctuary, conventional thought is so easy. One should do this and that, talk this way, feel this way. Life is not so simple for those who have sacrificed to make possible those very conventions. Ethan Edwards, the consummate John Wayne hero, must ride away. He first rode away to defend the Southern rights to their land. Then he rode away after the war to work through his mission despite the sense of betrayal, and so that his anger might not pollute the homestead he left. He rides away with Martin to obtain justice and recover Debbie. In the very end, he must ride away because he no longer can exist within the conventional life. His home is beyond the sunset. He heads there like the beaten saint, crooked in walk like St. Paul must have been, troubled still in mind, but with integrity and vocation fully intact. He has lost everything—love, home, reputation, innocence—except the hope of heaven. He carries the burden of many killings; yet he knows his judge sees all. In the end, he hands Debbie over to the Nesby family who will tend her and raise her from there. And he may stop by some day down the road, but he is too large to stay long in that or any home. We saw this foreshadowed at the start in the opening scene at his brother's place, that Ethan is too big to stay. Aaron immediately questions Ethan how long the stay will be. Clayton, the pseudo big man in town, wonders the same. Ethan, the forever outsider, the one person with the courage to see the whole truth and put his convictions to the ultimate test, must remain silent now until he faces God, for the new homestead and new town can only exist with him as potency, not as fact.

Famously the final silhouette of Ethan in the doorway of the Nesby home has Wayne posture in a way that gives tribute to Harry Carey Sr., a familiar face from older Westerns who had died a few years before, and who had established early on the character of the Western hero as outsider and who starred in John Ford's first feature *Straight Shooting* (1917). Honor where honor is due. Ethan is a dead man as well, as he walks away slow and angular into the red landscape of the setting sun. Earlier he had mentioned that the cold weather was getting to his bones. There is a metaphor. When the truth becomes a legend, print the legend, goes the punchline for Ford's *The Man Who Shot Liberty Valance.* Ethan has folded into the legend. God's ways are mysterious, paradoxical: life is always precious, but salvation can only be achieved through death. The hero must lose his life to save it. And in losing his life, he saves others none as worthy as he.

*The Searchers* is a Christian tale. Paul the persecutor becomes the agent of heaven to preach the new gospel of grace. Love is now the transcendent reality. Love alone can change a man, conquer his hate, make his desolation turn fruitful. Ethan walks away so we can walk ahead, and thus the emotional force and continuing popularity of the film, despite the Marxists. We are Debbie and Martin and Clayton and the whole host of secondary characters, even the stock character of old Mose who is reduced to a simpleton after his suffering but who deserves that rocking chair on the porch as reward for his lonely trial. We live because these heroes came before us. We overcome our demons because other heroes fought and triumphed over theirs.

# 9

# BRIEF ENCOUNTER

*Is it true, prince, that you once declared that 'beauty would save the world'? Great Heaven! The prince says that beauty saves the world! And I declare that he only has such playful ideas because he's in love!*

—Fyodor Dostoyevsky, *The Idiot*

In 1999 when the British Film Institute published their list of the 100 best British films of the century, that group chose David Lean's *Brief Encounter* (1945) for number two, ahead of T*he 39 Steps* (1935), Olivier's *Henry V* (1944), *The Red Shoes* (1948), and *Lawrence of Arabia* (1962); behind only Carol Reed's *The Third Man* (1949). The BFI declaration troubled some who failed to understand or accept the moral assumptions driving Brief Encounter or who questioned the film's heavy dependence on its Rachmaninov score and the smallness of the production. The objections recalled those who overlook Tolstoy's moral tales in the light of his novels, discounting uniqueness in form and so overlooking Pope's dictum,

*A perfect judge will read each work of wit*
*With the same spirit that its author writ.*

*Brief Encounter* is not only one of the best British films ever made but one of the greatest works of world cinema, comparable to Kurosawa's *Rashomon* (1950), Ozu's *Tokyo Story* (1953), Bresson's *Pickpocket* (1959), and a film we will soon take up, Chaplin's *City Lights* (1931). In fact, *Brief Encounter* is among the most beautiful films ever made, a flawless gem of visual cinema, and as such a work of rare emotional power.

My argument begins with the telling side note that twice producers and directors made the fatal mistake of attempting to channel the power of Lean's masterpiece through their own lens, and both times the attempts proved consummate failures—Alan Bridges television version of 1974 with the same title and Ulu Grosbard's *Falling in Love* (1984) starring two icons of that era, Robert DeNiro and Meryl Streep. Remakes are rarely successful, and almost invariably so when the original depends on unique cinematic and narrative components.

The story for *Brief Encounter* derives from the short Noël Coward play *Still Life* (1935), written as part of a cycle of ten slice-of-life plays to be performed across three evenings. Two ordinary married people meet by chance in a train station, and then meet again by chance later in the day in a small village, and then meet again the following week only to find themselves unexpectedly in love, and in the kind of love only troubadours and poets describe well. The woman, Laura Jesson, from whose point of view the story is told, suffers most in the unfolding of the relationship, because she is married to a good, if a bit dull, man, and they have two young children. The man, a doctor named Alec Harvey, also has two children, both boys, and a comfortable marriage to his small and dark wife, his description. We never get a glimpse into Alec's home but take it for a dimmer mirror of Laura's, comfortable and conventional. As Laura and Alec progress in their relationship, which covers only a month and is never consummated, Laura grows increasingly troubled by the lies and deceit involved. When caught by acquaintances in an awkward attempt to cover up the affair, Laura determines that she and Alec must give it up. They arrange for one final day together and then part at the train station, Alec to travel to South Africa where he will take up a new medical practice, Laura to return her husband and ordinary suburban life. Both will be forever changed and perhaps for the worst.

In the above list of the masterpieces, *Brief Encounter* most resembles Ozu's *Tokyo Story* (1953). The affair between Alec and Laura goes on nearly unnoticed by those who observe; yet, the emotions involved run so very deep—in both films the stories end with the main characters looking down a long road of uncertainty and loneliness. This eventuality is suggested in Lean's first scene in which we see from a distance Alec and Laura huddled together in the refreshment room of the train station, the camera acknowledging their presence, but drawn instead to action in the foreground, a petty lovers' quarrel between a ticket collector, Albert Godby, and the counter woman, Myrtle Bagot. As the scene progresses, the camera slowly, almost reluctantly, moves off the lovers quarreling to the silent couple at the table. Then before we can gather what is transpiring, an intrusive and loud acquaintance of Laura's spots them and begins to chatter away. What we will discover by the end of the film is that under the noise and restrained demeanors of Alec and Laura, this moment of pending departure is crushing them. A later scene reprising the event reveals that Laura is contemplating throwing herself like Anna Karenina under the express.

The quiet power under the surface of the images and actions is part of the mystique of *Brief Encounter*. Over and again we hear an echo of Wordsworth's "Oh, the difference...." All seems so unremarkable—the station, the many passengers, the familiar employees, the conversation, and even the main players, two middle-aged people waiting quietly for the trains that will return them home. Neither of the two leads, Celia Johnson and Trevor Howard, draw the camera by their glamour, although both were known film veterans and consummate performers. But under this seeming commonplace, passions stir that rival those in any Shakespearean tragedy. Laura nearly does throw her life away, and Alec may be acting out the same by moving across the globe to Johannesburg.

Thus, *Brief Encounter* reveals itself to be a deeply philosophical work. The message is of the tragedy of humankind, "Fate" Laura will term it late in the plot. Her term of despair suggests a cynicism one finds in Thomas Hardy's "Hap" in which "purblind Doomsters" toy with innocent people:

> *—Crass Casualty obstructs the sun and rain,*
> *And dicing Time for gladness casts a moan. . .*
> *These purblind Doomsters had as readily strown*
> *Blisses about my pilgrimage as pain.*

However, if this story of Laura and Alec were suggesting such a grim and cold universe, the resolution when Laura returns to her husband Fred is all wrong. Of all the scenes that bring us to tears in this poignant story, that last reconciliation scene might be the most powerful. We will get to this in detail. For now, suffice it to say that the ending is not grim, but profoundly human. Fred is a good man, and Laura does love him, and she is glad she has returned home in the end. What is at work here is not Fate, but life in a fallen world redeemed only by divine mercy.

A better reflection upon *Brief Encounter* suggests the gospel story of the woman caught in adultery more than it does Hardy's and Laura's bitter suggestion. Let he who is without sin cast the first stone. Neither Laura nor Alec chooses in a premeditated way to enter an intimate relationship, nor do they plan to fall in love so hopelessly. They each make missteps that leave them vulnerable, but the film suggests, and we understand, that the unexpected calamity just naturally occurs once the first seemingly innocent moves are made. As Laura tells the story in a long flashback from the train that takes her back home after she parts from Alec the last time, she tries to piece together how it all came to pass, the way a physician or counselor might. She provides us a careful itinerary of times and dates and places and her initial and subsequent impressions. When her intrusive and talkative friend, Dolly Messiter, asks who Alec is after he leaves, Laura responds almost to herself, "I hardly know him at all." And her expression indicates her words ring true to herself.

It is important to stress that physical attraction is not what draws the two lovers together, though each finds pleasure in the presence of the other. This, of course, is why the Richard Burton and Sophia Lauren version of the film works so poorly, assuming by virtue of the casting something fundamentally untrue about human affection, that it *must* be driven by human passion. What draws Alec and Laura is a complementary quality of mind and character, a common sense of humor, a hidden desire for life to be more luminous than it presently is for either. Alec's first compliment to Laura is "You are too sane and uncomplicated" followed by "You could never be dull." He needs sane and uncomplicated, hinting that home does not provide him with either. The anonymity of the place where they meet is a critical factor, the town of Milford where Laura goes shopping on Thursdays and where Alec has one extension of his practice. Their love affair recalls the common experience of camp romance or perhaps one teased when travelling; several other films with similar premises come to mind—*An Affair to Remember*, *A Room with a View*, and notoriously Lina Wertmüller's *Swept Away*.

The mystery of human affection and love. Why this person instead of that? The equal mystery of divine love. Why does Zacchaeus leap down from the tree or Nicodemus visit when his peers will not? No dull sermon has ever helped us understand. All we know really is that these things happen, and when they happen it is often without warning, and certainly without a guidebook. The story of *Brief Encounter* is no morality tale warning us to be more prudent, though it does leave some of that impression. The story drives home the reality that such things can happen no matter how hard people try to be good, and when they do happen, it is a sad circumstance, one that inevitably leaves the bitter truth that some wisdom is only achieved through suffering. Laura suffers deeply in the story and will continue to suffer after the final curtain falls. Christ have mercy on her soul. The idea comes through the Noel Coward source material, which echoes Chekhov's short story "The Lady with the Dog." In that famous tale a bored Russian bureaucrat picks up a similarly bored younger woman while on a vacation in Yalta only to find himself in love with her when he returns home to Moscow. The two consummate the affair and conspire to meet when possible out of sight. In the end in a muted scene, the man passes a mirror in some hotel room and notices his hair graying; then he consoles his mistress who has been in despair over her intuition that the lovers can never come out of the shadows. Life carries the seeds of tragedy and comedy, and we should respect both when they arrive, and how they arrive. As in Hardy, we blame cruel fate in the Chekhov world. Far less so in the world conjured by Coward and Lean.

Beyond the unforgettable articulation of this bittersweet truth, the film's distinguishing mark is the Rachmaninov score, his *Piano Concert in C Minor* (1900), one of the greatest pieces of the twentieth century, a dazzling, emotional masterwork that takes the best of the nineteenth-century romantic tradition and blends it with a prophetic sorrow that seems to presage the coming collapse of Russia and calamity which would become the twentieth century.

The Rachmaninov concerto controls the emotional movement of the film from the opening credits. It creates the context with which the viewer can understand all the key dramatic moments. It even enters the story directly in the final sequence as Laura puts on a record while sitting with Fred and ruminating over the tragedy of the past month's events. The concerto becomes her metaphor, communicating the tragedy that Laura will never be able to tell her story in real time to the souls near her sphere, and especially to the one closest to her, the devoted husband. Nothing in the history of film matches the integration of that single piece of music through this one film. Whereas the emotional effects have tended to cast *Brief Encounter* as classic melodrama, it may be more accurate to align it with the musical genre. Melodrama regards characters thrust into often improbable situations that heighten the emotions involved, whereas *Brief Encounter* tells of believable characters thrust into a highly probable situation, at least one which all mature souls should recognize and make the sign of the cross. The music does not force the emotion like a laugh track in a situation comedy. It runs alongside the action in perfect harmony, and it allows the viewer to step out of the flow of ordinary narrative time into a realm almost mystical. There are no scenes in which the music seems arbitrary and manipulative. In fact, there are a couple of scenes—such as Laura running through the rain and then wandering the streets in despair after leaving Alec near the conclusion—where the music provides the film's dialogue as much as Laura's own narration has. The music communicates what she, and we, have no words to express properly.

This is where *Brief Encounter* can become very personal. My mother loved Rachmaninov and played her recording loud many late summer afternoons when she sat in her chair grieving her failed romance with my father and the desperation of her own circumstances. I recall returning home as a boy from some afternoon of games to hear Rachmaninov drifting through the open windows of our corner house and her weeping inside.

The perfection of Lean's film does not address only the emotional force provided through the Rachmaninov concerto, although that masterpiece and the film become inseparable once experienced together. Every scene from first to last has a rare clarity. The film only runs 88 minutes. The DeNiro Streep remake *Falling in Love* runs 106 minutes. That says a lot. Every aspect of *Brief Encounter* under scrutiny comes to resemble a detail in something as remarkable as Vermeer's Girl with a Pearl Earring. This shot, this blocking of performers, this angle cannot be otherwise. There is a luminosity of the whole that conveys an almost otherworldly coherence.

The initial title scene sets up everything to follow and illustrates the point. A train station at night in a dark fog. We hear the screeching of metal, danger, the smoke of a passing train billowing softly through the night sky; and then the music begins. Trains have a mystique. Who is riding on them? Where are they heading? The heads and partial figures speed past leaving only an impression of life, color, and shape. We want definition. Instead we are offered an impression of romance and danger, the twin subjects of the story, something threatening that might carry us to some faraway place, yet one of allure. The shot lingers on the space the train has left behind, a tower, tracks leading who knows where, dim lights suggesting security on the platform, but limited. Another train approaches, heading toward us this time, it's whistle cutting through the music. On the platform, a ticket collector checks his watch and is assured, but of what, of time? Time seems so fixed when observed on a watch but is experienced in so liquid a fashion in life. For two of those whom we will find inside, time is proving a cruel enemy. Another cut provides us an overhead view of this train, the express, blasting through the station. No certainty in this image, just threat and danger, a foreshadowing.

The elements are all there—transition, intrigue, false domesticity, presumption, romance, danger, wisdom, folly, the beauty and romance of the night.

The collector crosses over the tracks and takes us inside the refreshment room where we are greeted with the shrill voice of the matron, Myrtle, "Good evening, Mr. Godby." He leans carefree across the counter and responds in kind, "Hello, hello, hello." Nothing to see here; however, the voices and manners are out of step with the powerful images we have been presented outside the room. Something misses the tone in the pitch and timbre of those voices, a motif played throughout the film. Laura's voice when it comes is lovely and modulated. Alec's is rich and refined. Not so the secondary characters. One wonders how the suggested Keatsian high romance of the opening notes can be played out in such a setting with such characters passing across the stage. After lines of idle chatter from the two at the counter, the camera pans to that table in the corner where the lovers sit together. They wear common clothes, he in a professional coat, she dressed for a day out. He, like Albert though restrained, leans in toward her, stirring his tea reassuringly, while she stares down into her cup motionless. The chatter from the counter spills over this quiet scene, mocking it. Then to further the effect, we cut back to the two at the counter continuing what becomes evident as a flirtatious exchange. When another cut returns us to the table, just as we begin to note the solemn expressions on the lovers' faces, in bursts the new character, evidently an acquaintance of

Laura, Dolly, carrying parcels and in a flurry of movement and words, glad to have made the station on time. Alec looks at Laura in a way that suggests this entrance a cruel annoyance. Laura then introduces Alec, and Dolly takes the opportunity to send him to the counter for more tea. Turning back to Laura, leaning in, she lays the impression out, "My dear, what a nice-looking man. Who on earth is it? Really, you're quite the dark horse. I shall telephone Fred in the morning and make mischief." Laura sits back and can't find words. There it is in the crassest of terms, the whole affair hinted and its inevitable consequence.

The dramatic action is triggered by the sound of the train bell, a motif throughout the film. "There's your train," Laura says to Alec. It is so common a line but not here, life and death here. So also, when moments later Alec gets up to leave and presses Laura's shoulder gently to mask the truth from their unwanted guest.

Then follows the climactic moment, though not to be explained until later. The action occurs off screen. Laura's talkative friend Dolly goes to the refreshment counter for chocolate, and when she looks back Laura is gone. "Where is she?" Laura enters and leans back into the door looking haggard and unwell. They bring her brandy. "I feel a little sick," Laura says. Celia Johnson's performance throughout the sequence is one of the wonders of the film. How do you play a woman who has just gone to the edge of a train platform to commit suicide, as we discover later, and then backed out of it, who is trying to cover the fact to strangers who have no idea what has just transpired, and whom she would never tell in a thousand years?

Once Laura gets on her train home with Dolly, the explication begins via Laura's languorous voiceover as she looks away from her companion chattering away and speaks her thoughts directly to the viewers, we who are unseen and so safe. "This can't last. This misery can't last."

Laura's initial painful musings are mirrored later in the film when giddy from her first kiss from Alec, she returns home seeing in the train window images of a teenage fantasy of her and Alec dancing at some fine event and travelling to exotic places. We know that fantasy life cannot last either. This later scene will blend into another with Laura in her bedroom applying makeup though it is dinner time, staring blissfully into her vanity and lying to Fred for no good reason that she had lunched with an old friend, Mary Norton. It was the beginning of a set of easy lies, though not easy in consequence. She will have to call Mary Norton for cover, and then on the following Thursday will be spotted by Mary and a winking friend at a fine restaurant drinking champagne with Alec. To maintain the lies means to assent to the loss of her soul, to follow the piper down the lane to some dangerous place where home will be only a distant echo.

As the affair unfolds, and mercifully never brought to its conclusion, Laura feels more shame than bliss. She comes home late one night to find her son has been struck by a car and is in bed with a concussion. Raymond Carver will reprise that idea in his short story "A Small Good Thing," though there the boy will die; here Laura's son mercifully recovers. Still, she takes it as a sign, as she does the fact that she cannot get from her mind the echo of Mary and her friend playing along. When Laura and Alec return to a country bridge where they had stopped and embraced earlier, there is no joy. "We leaned down" toward the water, Laura tells us, but "Happy? No, not really." As the day pushes forward, the two grow more silent; long lost is the chatty camaraderie of their first meetings. Both realize the relationship must come to a resolution, so Alec tells her that night at the station that he is going back to the friend's apartment where he is staying. He has the key, and Stephen will be gone that evening. Laura hurries to the train and attempts to go home but cannot. She hurries back to meet Alec at the apartment, carried along by the tense undulations of the Rachmaninov score.

Her trip to the apartment brings all the visual and auditory elements together around the theme of the relationship with Alec as a trap. It is night. Laura is alone, no tenants or passersby as she enters the apartment building. It has been raining, and she is in a state. All the windows inside have cross bars, and we see Laura against them and through them. As she climbs to the flat, the camera stays back viewing her through a barred open area. We don't know her anymore. She is in the process of losing herself. She stands motionless facing the closed door of the flat.

When the door opens, Alec is pleasantly surprised to find her having returned, and his look confirms something played subtly throughout. There is a touch of smug triumph in it. Alec was the truly unhappy one at the start of the story. He rose to take a speck from Laura's eye in the initial scene at the station when they meet, and he plants a beam there in its stead. He compliments Laura, a married woman, at their first lunch and insists they meet again. He is the pursuer and she the prey, though he never acknowledges it. He presses her after they go boating, insisting she face the truth of their love, "You know what's happened, don't you? I've fallen in love with you." In the end, he flees to South Africa leaving her to her grief and near suicide. He acts and she receives, and he seems to act with intention, whereas she is drawn in, so our sympathies reach to her rather than him—the moral equation favors Laura. In the apartment he insists she take off her things and sit. We know what that suggests. It comes as welcome relief when his friend Stephen arrives back early and hears Laura hurrying away down the back. She leaves her scarf behind which Stephen will hand to Alec and follow with a request for the return his latchkey, and a rebuke. Though Alec will try to defend himself and his wounded vanity that the situation is not "vulgar," the fact of the matter is that the situation is vulgar. Alec has used his friend's apartment as a space for the consummation of his seduction of a married woman, and he deserves the disgust he receives.

Laura's flight from the near adultery at Stephen's apartment eventuates on a bench in a square where a police officer will notice her lingering and question her intentions. More shame for Laura who has nowhere to go and no one to speak with, a painful moment worthy of Dickens or Hugo but cast in middle-class comfortable terms. Here the Rachmaninov score functions less to describe her hidden passions than to tease her by its contrast. This sordid conclusion is what she always guessed would happen, not the promised end of a high romance. The shame has nothing to do with puritanical attitudes either. She has walked out of her common life into a bourgeois tragedy, and Flaubert would have despised her as much as his own heroine. In fact, whereas Emma Bovary is foolish, Laura has sense, which makes matters even worse. Or, following another literary cross-reference, where the still young and radiant Anna Karenina is stuck in a stale, semi-arranged marriage to an older politician and therefore sympathetic, Laura has a good man and two decent children at home. What will crush her most at the end is that she realizes her best friend has always been her husband, and now she can never tell him the story because it would hurt him undeservedly.

This brings the events full circle. In the opening scene in the train station, Albert is teasing Myrtle and she resisting in her pinched way. As the story unfolds, it becomes clear that these two are also having an affair, but of the type in which Albert will see Myrtle bent over and slap her on the behind—not quite in keeping with Laura's dreamy ideal. The young girl working with Myrtle has her moment in the story as well, where she is being teased at night by two boys interested in testing her modesty. Both the girl and Myrtle have Cockney accents, and so Laura looks upon these common flirtations with a critical eye. We understand this from an earlier scene in which she and Alec enjoy a laugh at an awkward woman trying too hard to be a musician in both a restaurant and a movie theater. Yet in the end, Alec's sophisticated seduction leads Laura toward the same outcome—coarse jesting.

During their last day together, Alec rents a car, and the two conspirators drive in the fashion of sad lovers in any Hollywood movie, little talk and with Laura lighting Alec's cigarettes as they speed along. He has arranged this last day to lessen the pain, he says, but the pain is only increased for Laura: "I want to die. If only I could die," this after he tells her he loves her with all his heart and soul. One great mercy in the story is that Laura's practicality, her being uncomplicated as Alec tells her, makes her vulnerable to the escapist nature of the temptation, but it also saves her in the end. She is not a romantic like Emma Bovary or Anna Karenina or even Edna Pontellier in the Kate Chopin novel; she is afraid to kill herself. Also, she retains in the back of her mind the image of home, Fred, and the children. She loves them, too, and cannot block them out and hurt them so badly. That would be madness and a cruelty unspeakable.

All comes together in the most beautiful scene in the film, her return to home and Fred. Laura is in her chair suffering her long, sad reverie, having completed her story to us, the secret listeners. Fred has been quietly working a puzzle across from her, though he has inquired of her mood and gazed across curiously once when she was deep into her mood. Does he suspect? It would seem he does, though she mistook his silence for ignorance. He looks at her long and hard, with compassion and concern, and then goes to her, dropping to one knee and leaning in tenderly, not as Alec had done in his pursuit, but as a husband and friend, "Laura? Whatever your dream was, it wasn't a very happy one, was it?" "No."

This moment in the story may be the clearest emblem of the love and heaven at subject in this book. She is the wayward spouse, and he is not at fault. Her sad journey into the dark wood has left her lost and miserable. Will he judge? Does he have the right? Yes. However,

*The Lord is compassionate and merciful: longsuffering and plenteous in mercy.*
*He will not always be angry: nor will he threaten forever.*

"Is there anything I can do to help?" Fred continues. She deflects, "Yes, Fred, you always help." But he follows with a response that all of us who have ever been deeply wronged need to keep fixed in mind, "You've been a long way away. Thank you for coming back to me." She breaks into tears, and they embrace, the music punctuating this moment of grace with the most famous segment of the Rachmaninov score, the crescendo made popular in the 1945 popular song by Buddy Kaye, "Full Moon and Empty Arms." The moon is full outside, but the arms are not empty as Laura has found in the sorrow of harsh experience the man who truly loves her body and soul. We who have followed her journey alongside have likewise had revealed the truth always there hidden in plain sight. Fred's love was always there in plain sight.

So honest and human a movie compels certain questions. How often have we been spared the anguish of our own naivete and rash decisions by some sudden intervention of merciful providence? Laura has been spared. Have we as well? A phone call that did not go through. A friend who, like Stephen, dropped by at the most inconvenient moment. We do not understand the workings of heaven, but in the cool light of day upon reflection, we all must acknowledge that there is a gentle hand behind it all.

Further, we ponder those whom we know and love who fell seemingly without a net of protection. The dark enemy at our side asserts that the "purblind Doomsters" are having their way again and that our sense of providence is mere accident of nature, but we know better. Our hearts have been stirred. In those golden moments when we know we are loved in some strange, impossible way, Fred's words to Laura whisper to us, "and so are you forgiven, too, and loved, and so do I also rejoice in your return." Despite it all, carrying the shame of it all, yes. Cowper's old hymn captures the idea,

*Behind a frowning providence*
*He hides a smiling face.*

There will be lingering sorrow even so. But that sorrow has its own beauty as it leads to wisdom and sanctity. Alec and Laura have been drawn by forces that mocked their conventional lives, and those lives needed to be mocked to some degree. After the boy had his accident, Laura tells us that she and Fred began planning for his future—the navy perhaps. But he is just a boy, and what do the parents really know of the hidden secrets of his boyish heart? We hardly know what is in our own hearts. Life is mysterious and beautiful, and because beautiful dangerous and fragile. There is a power in love that should not be awakened until the right time. "I adjure you, O daughters of Jerusalem, that you not stir up or awaken love until it pleases" (Song of Songs 8: 4). Love is not tame but wild. C. S. Lewis reminds us likewise that God is not tame, but He is good. Both Laura and Alec enter the story with a diminished view of the wonder of the universe, and the diminished view of the love which drives all. By the end, they see much more. In fact, they begin to see more even before the end, though it takes the conclusion of the affair for the truth to be fully framed. In an earlier scene as the bond between the lovers begins to take on a new element, Alec tells Laura his desire to begin practicing preventive medicine, and she exclaims that just then he sounded like a little boy. So innocent and vulnerable and loveable. Love finds its source in something beyond the conception of those preoccupied with "getting and spending," as ever-old Wordsworth put it. We are moved by the eagerness of Laura's face as she speaks this, while also warned of the coming sordid but inevitable end of it all. Alec is unlawfully awakening a precious thing, genuine and deep, but made rather for the forest and field and quiet, private places, a fiercely jealous created thing.

Then there is the parting scene between Alec and Laura. Many private matters cannot be resolved in this life. Our sorrows spring from this source as well. I know a man who lost his son to drugs, who had little part of his son's life, but who grieves him every day, who lives their life together every day in his mind as it might have and should have been. In his grief, a grief that some might term irrational given the circumstances of the case, that man longs for heaven, a place beyond time and mortal logic that allows true reversals and rewrites. Shakespeare said his lover lived always in his sonnets, but this was a metaphor for how memory holds our treasures. Love does not live on in paper in words; and, sadly, even memory lets us down. Memory is liquid; it edits, enhances, and reshapes. Only heaven crafts a restored, redeemed vision. In heaven there is no marriage and giving in marriage, so should both Alec and Laura arrive, what would be the circumstance? Their genuine love could not be denied, so what form would it take beyond the lawful restrictions of this fallen earth? The one thing we know for sure is that heaven is boundless and ever pure. In heaven there will be no tears, for a visible mercy will rule from the throne.

We end with the Rachmaninov concerto once again. The *Concerto in C Minor* beckons us from the concrete and plastic reality of the modern world into one much more sublime. The ever-expanding arcs of the melody line drawn from the initial bittersweet F-minor bell toll, a melody echoed by oboe, flute, and French horn playing alongside the rich strings of the orchestra driven along by the insistence of the piano—the music affirms a kind personality governing the universe. The music presents us an intimate call that demands an intimate response. Rachmaninov drew this wonder from the well of his own personal suffering, and it evokes the deepest aches in those who hear.

In the film the music awakens us to something clean and simple: sorrow comes in broad and relentless waves even into the lives of the ordinary, like Laura, as it does to those with surprising depths, also like Laura. Sorrow proves the mother of all and the lover of all. When the film ends, we settle back into the commonplace expressions of our worlds but affirmed in our deepest hope that mercy is extended to us, too. We look through drying tears at the seeming ordinary and believe that the arms of the truly extraordinary have been extended toward us.

The time has come, Alec tells Laura as he offers her soft but final words, she leaning out the train window to capture the last breeze of fortune, embracing her lover without embracing him, both knowing that the affair has run out of time. "Forgive me?" Alec asks. "Forgive you for what?" "For everything. For meeting you in the first place... for taking a piece of grit out of your eye... for loving you... for bringing you so much misery." In this glowing moment, we forgive him as well. She offers her reply echoing the admonition from the Lord's Prayer. "I'll forgive you if you forgive me." The train starts away, and the camera leaves us to her longing, loving, suffering eyes.

# 10

# A FAREWELL TO ARMS

*Three things come together in heavenly fruition — perfect vision, full embracing, and the clinging of consummated love.*

—Thomas Aquinas,
*Commentary on the Sentences of Peter Lombard*

For film lovers who share a bias for very simple stories visually told, the works of Frank Borzage and his peer directors in the 1930s argue theirs being the golden age of film. Borzage loved a simple story, and particularly a simple love story. His filmmaking style was lush and evocative, full of metaphor and deep explorations into the hidden mysteries of the human heart. His best films remain long in the memory.

Frank Borzage was most influenced by German romanticism which he mingled with his cultural Catholicism, and those two together inclined him toward a filmmaking that pitched transcendent ideals over against harsh existential realities. Though his own personal faith remains an open question, his work falls solidly into an arena where people of more traditional faith find him quite companionable. *A Farewell to Arms* (1932) might well be a Church-approved treatise on the theological virtues of Christian marriage. It certainly stands as one of the most moving early films on the effects of intimacy on the soul, and as such finds a secure place here in this discussion of films that affirm our inner longings for love and heaven.

Borzage made *A Farewell to Arms* during his most productive years in which he successfully served Paramount (1932), Columbia (1933-34), Universal (1933), Warner Brothers/First National (1934-37), and Metro Goldwyn Mayer (1937-42). Many of his films at the time were anti-war or anti-fascist productions, most notably *A Farewll to Arms*, *Three Comrades* (1938), and the classic *The Mortal Storm* (1940). All posed war as destroyer of love and friendship, an indomitable force driven by faceless bureaucracies and demonstrating the world's indifference to the things of God. Resolution in these films, as in Borzage's silent classics, *Seventh Heaven* (1927) and *Street Angel* (1928), is achieved as the main characters recognize that their very human, earthly hopes can only be achieved fully in the new, better world to come.

Over Borzage's long and illustrious career, first as an actor in the early days of the silents, and then as a director once he had achieved success in 1920 with his *Humoresque*, he tended toward the popular domain of the melodrama; yet, his films never devolved into rank sentimentality. Borzage's genius was grounded in the sleight-of-hand that carries his often-predictable plots away from the maudlin into the immediate; that is, he transformed nineteenth-century Victorian plots into vehicles for much deeper levels of Catholic piety, and piety played out across the background of an incomprehensible, cold, modern world. This is well illustrated in the films of his great creative period, 1932-34, when he directed *Secrets*, *Man's Castle*, and our subject, *A Farewell to Arms*.

The melodramatic story form tends to posit absolutes, either/or juxtapositions of good versus evil, hope and despair, prosperity and poverty, age and youth. As in many other popular formulas, plots designed around such absolutes tend to work against the other artistic merits of a work, since the verisimilitude of the storyline strains the credulity of critical viewers. It's a good film, but I couldn't believe character x.... However, in Borzage's melodramas, these absolute juxtapositions find surprising variations that become compelling when placed within his highly evocative, transcendent frames. Somehow his characters remain real even when yanked hard into the most desperate of circumstances, and even when the Christian ideals of love and holiness the characters begin to represent become overt. And even when the surrounding cinematography makes the ideals rather obvious.

Borzage's tendencies made him a curious choice to adapt the source material of *A Farewell to Arms*, Ernest Hemingway's grim and cynical war novel published to acclaim three years before. Hemingway's fictional worlds in a very real way are tragic extensions of the suicide that would end his own life. Few who knew the novel *A Farewell to Arms*, who settled into the soft cushions of their local theater in 1932, could have imagined the transformation to be played out before them—the angst of the novel, seminal stuff for Lost Generation devotees, is redeemed by Catholic sacramentalism.

In a fashion, Borzage rewrote the Hemingway novel as he imagined the root story in its purest form, still tragic but far from pointless. The exercise parallels what Barry Levinson did in *The Natural* to Bernard Malamud's source material, except here the religious vision exudes from all the pores of the film, not just those of the concluding sequence. Instead of Hemingway's aimless war and arbitrary killings, we get war as emblem for the great struggle of humankind in a fallen world. Hemingway leaves us with cold rain and an indifferent sky. Borzage takes us on a passion journey toward a cleansing, sacramental rain; he defeats the darkness with bright light breaking through a dismal, muted background. Hemingway's characters are desperate, trying to grab hold of what little illusory happiness they can; Borzage's characters are focused toward the singular goal of making permanent their love through heroic virtue. Hemingway's plot is deeply cynical, Borzage's is deeply optimistic.

Paradoxically, Borzage's *A Farewell to Arms* remains reasonably faithful in detail to the Hemingway plot. Frederic Henry, an American medic serving with the Italian Red Cross in the First World War, falls in love with an English nurse, Catherine Barclay, who is being pursued by Frederic's closest friend, the surgeon Rinaldi. When Frederic is wounded by random artillery that lacerates his legs as he is in his barracks biting into a piece of cheese, Rinaldi arranges for him to stay in a hospital in Milan, where Catherine is serving, a casual gesture, one man of the world to another. What Rinaldi does not realize is that Frederic and Catherine have really previously fallen in love, consummated their relationship, and been married privately in the Roman Rite by a compassionate priest who pities them. When Frederic is released from the hospital and sent back to the front, Catherine leaves her position to move nearer to Switzerland, where she sends him daily letters in the hopes of a reunion once he serves his duty. However, Rinaldi, ignorant of the tenderness of the relationship and the priest's blessing, intercepts the letters so Frederic can get over her, which prompts Frederic to desert to go find Catherine and establish a life together in some neutral place. In the meantime, Catherine discovers she is pregnant and begins to experience complications. When the baby is delivered stillborn, Catherine hemorrhages and begins to fail. Frederic finds her in the hospital only in time for them to reaffirm their love, which they both acknowledge will last forever. She dies in his arms.

Life from death, hope from sorrow, intimacy from absence—the great themes that define the Christian faith, all present in the frames of Borzage's film. The opening images of the film cue us to see matters in this way. The standard Paramount credit sequence rolls over a patriotic, militaristic soundtrack punctuated with the sounds of bombs dropping. Then the music shifts to a romantic melody and orchestration typical in the Hollywood style, except the sounds of bombs continue. A title card follows celebrating "high on the rolls of glory" two names, the Marne and the Piave, cites of decisive Allied victories, though the film itself will not move in the direction of celebrating the triumph of one force against another, political good versus evil. The music then turns sweet and pastoral as the camera drifts over a quiet rural landscape, pausing only momentarily over the body of a soldier lying dead and unnoticed on a hillside. The camera continues on to a line of medical vehicles proceeding indifferently down a dirt road. All the images and sounds are contradictory, and thus the theme of the film is set. We will move between the polarities separating anonymity and intimacy, death and life, indifference and deep compassion.

Five characters are fully defined in the film, each serving an important thematic function. Frederic and Catherine, the young lovers, find a meaning to their lives through their love and commitment. He will desert the army to find her in Switzerland oblivious to the personal cost. She will leave the security of her hospital position to be with him and to mother the child she is carrying, even though it means living in impoverished circumstances. In the Hemingway novel, their love provides the only meaning amidst the chaos of war: "Why, darling, I don't live at all when I'm not with you," Catherine tells him. Borzage makes of their love, their tender words, their expressions, not responses to the desperation of life in a meaningless world amidst a pointless war, but an emblem of transcendence. Their love is pure and permanent. It wipes away the elements of war and all the scars of their past lives., but then it goes further and lifts them to a heroic stature, eventually making Catherine's death a martyrdom to holiness. Catherine does not die because the world lacks meaning but because the quality of love the lovers share is meant for another realm.

Two characters stand in counterpoint to Frederic and Catherine: the surgeon Rinaldi and Catherine's nurse friend, Miss Fergusson. Rinaldi and Fergusson are both bitterly pessimistic. Rinaldi tells Frederic in response to the revelation of his commitment to Catherine, "Sacred subjects are not good for soldiers. Why don't you be like me—all fire and smoke and nothing inside." Rinaldi's profession as surgeon is a metaphor for his biological view of life. At one point he tells Frederic of an operation in which he held a patient's still-beating heart in his hand; in a way, he holds Frederic's heart in his hand since he becomes the barrier to the exchange of the lovers' letters. Rinaldi despises Frederic's change from callous to human, and despises Frederic in turn, at least until the end when the friends do reconcile—Rinaldi will provide him Catherine's location and a boat to get there. He had appreciated Catherine first, or at least he wanted to enjoy her first, and he feels their friendship betrayed, and further Rinaldi feels scorn for the meaning Frederic chooses to pursue in his devotion to Catherine, as that ordered love violates his own disordered nihilism. The war should not be redeemed in such a way. Fergusson shares a similar view and refuses to help Frederic locate Catherine when Frederic is in pursuit. She has earlier warned Catherine that the two lovers will either fight or die, as war brings all relationships to one or the other. Also, though a hidden motive, she was overlooked by Frederic when at the start Rinaldi offered her, one man to another, in exchange for Catherine. There is jealousy in her bitterness and passive revenge, though she hides it behind a cloak of sarcasm and feigned concern.

The fifth character who stands out from the narrative is the Italian priest who marries the lovers and offers his blessing to Frederic when he hears of the medic's planned desertion. Of all the players, he alone understands and bridges both the hopeful optimism of the two and the stark realism of Rinaldi and Fergusson. He stands in symbol as the Church, dispensing sacraments while withholding final judgment, and on a more practical level he provides the warmth of compassion and wisdom to characters desperately needing both. He does not encourage the lovers in their desperate course, but neither will he hinder them. Their humanity and the hope of their salvation depends on their freedom to choose a path forward, whatever the cost. He prays and blesses, and though potentially cast as a stock character, he stands out instead as the most fully human. In an exchange with Frederic in the hospital after Frederic is wounded, the priest brings mosquito netting, a bottle of vermouth, and English newspapers. Hardly a plaster saint there. Then he goes on to tell the wounded man that he "hates the war," but in a way different than Frederic who does "not mind it." The camera captures his distress in closeup. He understands the conflicts all together and overcomes them in his mind by the only means of grace that can overcome such evils. The priest's benediction speaks over the film and makes the ending both beautiful and inevitable.

One other character might be included here—the war itself. The war drapes the screen from side to side, from the opening image of an unknown soldier lying dead on a quiet hillside to the concluding images of bells ringing in the armistice. The war is the antagonist, teasing the main characters toward despair, swallowing up countless minor characters, and forcing the climactic choices which will prove salvific for all. The ringing church bells in the final sequence end the film's principal conflict, just as much as they suggest the divine response to the marriage promise Frederic and Catherine make at her deathbed. The images of the ringing church bells dissolve in one moment into that of a placard on a wall reading "Armistice Declared." No mention is made of Germans or Allies, but the final triumph is over war and death, society with a divine blessing over the chaos of hell.

What the war produces from the perspectives of the characters involved is a distortion of hope and values, and Borzage plays this theme throughout the narrative. Even in scenes where no bombs are dropping in the background, the movement of soldiers and passersby on the street appears a congested rush in all directions at once. At the start of the film, the chaos has become part of Frederic's general attitude. He shows indifference to men dying in an ambulance, rakishness to women he passes in the hospital, and drunkenness. He moves through spaces aimlessly. By the end of the story, he is freed from all three sins, and when he awaits news on Catherine's last progress through a cafe and hospital, he is framed in a more private and controlled way. While in the cafe, he prays for her recovery, and the camera lingers on his reverie for a full half minute, the longest single shot in the film.

Borzage projects a series of distorted images throughout the film to reinforce this aspect of the theme. Interior shots are invariably cramped with the camera rather too close to the subjects, and the backgrounds are in poor focus, dissected by odd visual lines and angles in the style of earlier German Expressionist film. Subjective camerawork suggests the insecure vision of both Frederic and Catherine as they are wheeled through halls in their hospital beds. Faces and lights come into their view unexpectedly to break the flow of the ceiling overhead. Borzage's camera maintains this visual subjectivity throughout the film, but never so overtly as in these point of view sequences. The frequent use of expressionistic devices—dissolves, high and low contrast lighting, skewed angles, unexpected camera positions—distort any semblance of viewer objectivity and compel a sympathy for these characters caught in so incomprehensible a world. All this changes, however, in the romantic scenes where Frederic and Catherine are imaged through filters and angelically from a fixed camera position, a visual technique used in melodrama but rarely with the transcendent power here. The war scenes are always shrouded in darkness, particularly in the long montage sequence of Frederic's initial pursuit of his love through enemy territory. The camera offers a similar darkness when it closes in on the anguished expressions of the lovers in moments of tension, as when Catherine watches Frederic leave to return to the front, or when Frederic worries over the absent letters from Catherine and fears for her life. For reinforcement, these intimacies are juxtaposed with more distanced and practical shots of Rinaldi or the other soldiers and nurses, with the notable exception of the soft-focus shots of the sympathetic priest who marries the lovers and blesses Frederic's journey to recover his love.

The film's most striking stylistic feature is the remarkable montage sequence of Frederic's journey from the Italian front to Milan in search of Catherine. Earlier he had mocked the indifference of God, finding a certain pleasure in recounting how his injury came while biting into some cheese. Here Frederic begins a journey fraught with peril that will culminate when Rinaldi, also freed from his disordered affections, sends Frederic by boat to Switzerland where he finally finds Catherine waiting. The sequence plays in sharp contrast to Frederic's original curse of defiance toward the war and life in general.

As this sequence encapsulates the overall conflict between love and war, Borzage uses it to anchor the film narrative—somewhat like a stand-alone and defining musical number in a Hollywood musical. It moves the action forward while providing the interpretive frame that simultaneously unlocks the story. The dominant feature of the montage is Frederic's incessant motion through the varying landscapes, whether alone or marching with troops and evacuated villagers, and always against the threatening gloom and rain. Punctuating the sequence are expressive images of suffering and death, especially the death of the innocent. A bandaged soldier stands in a slanted doorway, behind which is a large red Cross symbol, and stretches his arms Christlike. A graveyard of hundreds of crosses lingers on the screen. Telephone and electrical polls cast a shadowed "T" over the land. Soldiers march on. Frederic slips around and through the hurrying masses, falls to the ground to avoid exploding shells, leaps into a river to elude gunshots from the bank. The complete procession, which it is, places Frederic alternately in the position of the suffering Christ and the suffering Church. Most of the images are stylistically expressionistic, thus suggesting the psychological dysfunction and disorientation produced by the events. Frederic becomes Everyman on a pilgrimage through the valley of the shadow of death.

The rain which falls incessantly in the montage and throughout the film mimics the Hemingway ending where rain falling when Frederic leaves the hospital after Catherine's death functions as objective correlative for the hero's despair. Borzage broadens this to have the rain suggest nature's reaction to the madness unfolding across the land. The rain falls around the train platform as Frederic departs to the front; it falls throughout his journey to Milan and then Switzerland; it falls upon the streets outside the hospital as he waits in anguish the verdict regarding Catherine's fate in the end. Catherine has told him, "I hate the rain... I'm afraid of the rain." She sees in it the foreshadowing of her own death, the fulfillment of Fergusson's prophecy. A complementary device to the rain is that sound of distant bombs dropping throughout the story. The sound of the bombs, which punctuate the opening notes of the musical score, accelerates throughout the montage sequence. The Dragon is in pursuit of the Lady. Both symbols, rain and bombs dropping down destruction, find their answer in the final moments as Frederic lifts the dead Catherine from her hospital bed to the windows which open to sunlight and not bombs but the hopeful sound of bells.

In those final moments, the camera remains tenderly fixed alongside the lovers as they reaffirm that their commitment will remain forever. Frederic has Catherine repeat what is in effect their earlier private marriage vow, "In life, and in death, we will never be parted." She looks away from him, heavenward. "You do believe that, don't you Catherine?" "I believe it," she reaffirms, Wagner playing dramatically in the background. "And I am not afraid." She looks exultant and dies in his embrace. The bells cut through the music just then, followed by a boat horn, louder bells and the sounds of a jubilant crowd, the images dissolving one into the next. The camera remains in its respectfully fixed position as Frederic lifts her from the bed, the sheets flowing like a white wedding gown, and carries her reverently to the open window, sunlight glowing through tree branches. He raises his head, but not to the camera, which is capturing this from behind. "Peace. Peace," he says dramatically, completing the offering to the God who created their love. Had the shot been taken from the front, the effect would have been opposite, focusing on personal grief and hope. Here the camera offers certainty, Catherine handed over to the bells and the announcement of peace. Doves fly off into the distance. Frederic himself speaks the words of peace like a priest would with Wagner's "Liebstod" playing over his benediction. The souls of both are now set free. The offering has been made, a symbolic mass, the ritualistic offering of Christ for the love of his people. It completes the imagery of Frederic's passion journey. Death and destruction are no more.

The final scene stands alone as the ultimate incarnational moment of a decidedly religious film. Bells, the flight of the doves, the chorus of song, the gestures—all suggest that heaven and earth have come together. The story has found a divine conclusion, and we are invited to participate. It is also noteworthy that the rain has stopped, and Catherine's previously black window has been replaced with the tree branches reflecting light and gentleness. Death has been swallowed up by life.

This way this scene is shot and supported formally, the abrupt alteration of all previous manners of composition and all visual and auditory motifs, is common in the history of film where religious subjects are invoked. I will take this up in more detail in the conclusion to this collection. For now, it is worth noting that the narrative of *A Farewell to Arms* takes the elements of the Christian liturgy to its conclusion. The priest who plays such a key role in the earlier scenes might as well be in the background here with hands folded. The changed cinematic devices function as metaphor for the divine transformation of common elements. Both Frederic and Catherine are common after all. Neither exude a special grace. Though stars, neither Helen Hayes nor Gary Cooper who play the leads, had the aura of transcendent beauty and courage. They stand in for every set of lovers led by the circumstances of war to seal their contract of love without the typical preparations.

Yet stripped of those formalities, they are left with the two essential elements of the sacrament of marriage, and it is a sacrament in the film, a love that can only be explained as an act of God, and a commitment which is the highest of the acts of man.

Following this line of thought, Frederic's pilgrimage to Catherine is intended as a reflection of Christ's journey to Calvary to rescue his captive bride the Church. The montage is full of cross imagery. In one prominent shot a large crucifix leans at an acute angle toward the center of the landscape where a lone burnt tree, suggesting the crown of thorns, anchors the center of the composition, a Red Cross symbol on a structure behind it, darkness engulfing over half the remaining frame. Frederic travels through the valley of humiliation and suffering to find his bride. He challenges death while she awaits helpless in her condition, though she confesses at the end, "I knew you would come." As Catherine lies in the hospital bed awaiting surgery, she is shrouded in white with a nun-like covering for her head. Afterward, when Frederic is allowed to see her, the nurses have fixed her hair in simple waves that convey a virginal appearance, "I'll never stop loving you," Frederic tells her, "in life and death we will never be parted."

The Christian patterning of these moments resonates back over earlier scenes. Just prior to the deathbed sequence, Frederic retreats to a restaurant for coffee and a brioche. It is his Paschal meal, and he eats it with eyes looking deep into the nature of things. It stands in contrast to the meal of cheese he ate with his comrades when the bombs dropped. Likewise, the drink untouched before him contrasts with the easy flow of liquor in the beginning. The announcement of the war's end first comes during this scene, but the peace he hopes for is otherwise, "Oh God, don't let her die." We understand from the end that his prayer will be heard.

The priest has tremendous significance in this context. He appeared in three key scenes before. His first appearance follows Frederic's second meeting with Catherine during an air raid and immediately precedes the scene when the two consummate their love in a garden under the shadow of trees. In a hazy romanticized composition, the priest is surrounded by medics who mock his faith saying that he should not be troubled by the sound of bombs dropping because "What is death to a Christian?" Bearing a large black cross on the pocket of his uniform, the priest takes the banter with grace, placing a compassionate hand on the shoulder of the soldier who utters the jest. To emphasize the prominence of his position in the narrative, the camera remains in a fixed position allowing only the full face of the priest to be visible. The scene is purely thematic, with little plot function except to set the place for the meeting of Frederic and Rinaldi, wherein they plan for their night of pleasure with the nurses—Miss Barclay for Rinaldi and Miss Fergusson for Frederic. The emphasis placed on the brief conversation sets up the arc which builds toward Catherine's death, the displacement of the Christian in the world and the notice taken by heaven.

The second appearance of the priest is in the hospital room in Milan where Catherine is tending the recuperating Frederic. The priest enters with some useful items for Frederic: the mosquito netting, papers, and vermouth. In the ensuing conversation, he picks up the truth of the lovers' relationship from Frederic's mention of children. At this, in the most poignant moment of the film, he pauses and steps to the side where he begins to recite the marriage rite in Latin. He is haloed in a soft light while standing before a crucifix. A cut back to Frederic and Catherine reveals their understanding of the gesture and words, and they awkwardly straighten themselves and clasp hands. Frederic tells Catherine that he regrets the lack of orange blossoms, and organ music. She replies, "I can smell them… I can hear it plainly." Here again, the scene advances the plot but with a much richer significance. The true plot is playing out above and around the lovers, as it has been playing out for centuries.

The following appearance of the priest follows the same pattern. He is the friend Frederic chooses to entrust with the secret of his desertion and the reason for it, that Catherine's letters came back to him unopened. The setting is a dark exterior of the medical camp, with vehicles and soldiers passing ominously in the background. The two are depicted in heavy shadow, although light reveals Frederic's profile more distinctly. The priest hesitantly agrees to Frederic's request that his disappearance is not told until the morning, and that his friends are bid goodbye. Again, the significance of the scene resides in its thematic importance, for the episode triggers the lyrical montage of Frederic's journey to find Catherine. "What does this war mean to me anymore? What does anything mean, but finding her?" His desertion, when juxtaposed with the presence of the priest and ensuing montage, is recontextualized as a heroic pursuit, lover of the beloved, a pursuit worthy of a knight, but as familiar as Hawkeye under the waterfall telling Cora he will find her when the Indians spirit her away. He has not renounced the army but the world, and for a love marked as divinely favored. The priest reluctantly says goodbye and offers a blessing, "Goodbye, Frederico. May the Lord bless and preserve you."

Borzage's smoothly edited, highly filtered compositions, as this last encounter between Frederic and the kindly priest, tip off the viewers of *A Farewell to Arms* that the bleak storm of war with all its distortions, corruptions, and casualties can be softened and overcome by divine mercy. The romantic score of the film, as well as its placement against the action, likewise contradicts the painful events explicit throughout the story. Frederic is in a bar holding the foot of a prostitute and commenting on the pretty contours of arch and ankle, and then a bomb drops, and the ensuing chaos resolves as if through transportation, with him in an outdoor shelter holding the foot of Catherine. God has chosen him for something better. The mysterious trajectory of providence carries him from carnality to love, from cynicism to a living hope. Death will be swallowed up in victory.

Borzage's camera directs the narrative gently. It is the omniscient wisdom, not just revealing the action but offering us a lens of sympathy with which to understand it. When Catherine writes her first letter to Frederic from her Swiss apartment, she describes the room in elegant terms: "The bed is empire and fit for an empress." Meanwhile the camera pans the room to reveal the squalor. The scene is pure melodrama until Borzage adds the punchline of Catherine laughing to herself, pushing the letter into its envelope, and speaking to her distant lover that the lodgings are ugly and her heart lonely: "I'm an awful liar, darling. It's not really a nice place at all..." The clever maneuver transforms the action from the artificial to the bittersweet and tender, reminding us that these are ordinary people after all. Throughout the film, whenever the soft lens and evocative score totter against a coming tide of sentiment, Borzage redeems the moment with a visual and auditory tour-de-force, reestablishing credibility and genuine feeling—from the early battlefield scenes to the subjective shots as Frederic is wheeled into the hospital for surgery to the long montage of his journey to the pious ending.

As suggested earlier, crucial in understanding the artistic conception behind it all is to follow how Borzage reworks the Hemingway story to present an orthodox view of the marriage between the two principals. The

Church has long described marriage as an emblem of Christ's love for the Church. Christ loved her unto death. The heavenly bridegroom has departed only to prepare a suitable home where the lovers can share their joy forever. Marriage as an indissoluble bond because grounded in these metaphysical realities. Once Frederic and Catherine consummate their love, they are married in God's sight, and the priest merely seals the union through sacramental means. That Catherine bears his child follows naturally the sacramental union. And, as easily as the two principals fall in love and drift on soft clouds through its various stages, so easily do all who truly love discover a transcendent reality in the unfolding of the relationship. This is the underlying conception of the film. When Frederic lifts Catherine and carries her to the open window in the end, we are invited to join with our assent. The film is announcing the bans.

The foregrounding of the sacrament of marriage in Borzage's version of *A Farewell to* Arms makes its contrast with the Hemingway source novel so curious, Hemingway a nominal convert who moved unsteadily through four unhappy marriages. A likewise curious fact is that though raised Roman Catholic, Borzage became a high-ranking Freemason in the Scottish Rite, and, as all should know by now, Freemasonry is antithetical to the doctrines and practice of the Catholic faith. It is the subject of numerous encyclicals warning of its dire threat to the fabric of orthodoxy.

Such paradoxes used to trouble me until I studied years ago Pasolini's *Gospel According to St. Matthew* (1968). Pasolini was a practicing Marxist and a homosexual; yet, he created one of the most compelling film versions of the life of Christ, perhaps second only to Gibson's *Passion of the Christ* (2004). Pasolini was staying in a hotel in Assisi anticipating out of curiosity and perhaps some latent devotion a public visit from Pope John XXIII. While awaiting the event, the filmmaker happened upon a Bible in the hotel room and read the gospels from beginning to end, whereupon in the exaltation of his reading he was inspired to make the great film.

Life is as mysterious as the human soul.

# 11
# CITY LIGHTS

*Love hath so long possessed me for his own and made his lordship so familiar.*

—Dante Alighieri, *La Vita Nuova*

One of the more troubling aftereffects of the heavy Protestant influence in America, especially after the rise of revivalism in the nineteenth and early twentieth centuries, has been the general diminishing of the conception of heaven. The typical American Christian imagines heaven in modern, materialist terms—freedom from troubles, reacquaintance with lost family and friends, general ease, abundance. This cultural reality explains how an ideology as antithetical to historic Christianity as the prosperity gospel found any soft soil in which to take root. If heaven is imagined in material terms, then salvation must be measured and meted out in those same terms. We won the prize. God dispenses blessings when the right codes are typed into the machinery. For best access, add in exaggerated gestures and a few sanitized invectives in the fashion of the novice at a slot machine and the correct amount will be dispensed.

Such a conception of heaven would have provoked charges of blasphemy and heresy from gritty theologians like Augustine, Ambrose, Jerome, Anselm, and Thomas Aquinas. Counter-Reformational patriots like Loyola and Bellarmine would have added an even firmer nod of disapproval. Heaven is not to be understood in terms of what we get, although Scripture suggests the benefits will be beyond comprehension. It is to be understood in terms of our renewed relationship with God, a beatified vision—using the well-known expression of Aquinas, "perfect vision, full embracing, and the clinging of consummated love." The analogy can be found in the sacrament of marriage: it does lead to the conjugal bed and a measure of material and social stability and to immediate access to the ear of the beloved, but it is in essence a sacrament defined in that moment when man looks into the eyes of woman, both unveiled, both at the rapturous intersection of earth and heaven, mortality and immortality.

No single film depends upon this truth any more than Charlie Chaplin's masterpiece, *City Lights* (1931), and this chapter will provide both a detailed explication of that film and an apology for the now almost forgotten Church teaching regarding the significance of Christian marriage, and so by analogy the Christian conception of what heaven really entails. Our last discussion of Borzage's *A Farewell to Arms* illustrated the older conception of how lovers are positioned in pursuit of that goal. It also illustrated the otherworldly focus of the lovers. *City Lights* gets at the nature of the sacramental reality itself. The next chapter, a discussion of F. W. Murnau's *Sunrise*, will consider the contrast between true marriage and that which has been defined as marriage by modernity.

Now as with the Borzage film, *City Lights* suggests a paradox between the life of the auteur director and the implications of the director's art. Borzage was a Freemason; yet, his work seems quite Catholic. So, Chaplin was a known philanderer; yet, his work makes him out as a modern-day Don Quixote in pursuit of his Dulcinea, "There were no embraces, because where there is great love there is often little display of it." How to explain such paradoxes is beyond the margins of this book, but the paradoxes exist. Charlie Chaplin married four times. When he married his last wife, Oona O'Neill, daughter of the great playwright, he was 64 and she barely 18. Perhaps the secret is hidden in that latter fact. What we can say with certainty is that Chaplin's difficult upbringing equipped him to understand that material goods and social position are fickle blessings that can depart as quickly as they arrive, while true love, on the other hand, grows stronger and more permanent through adversity. Experience of the latter for Chaplin would indeed come through Oona who would bear him eight children and provide support through his numerous lawsuits, income tax challenges, and the ostracization caused by his political views.

Chaplin's upbringing in London offered more than a fair share of poverty and hardship. His ne'er do well father kept the family in constant financial straits, as with Dickens, leading to the boy's deposition in a workhouse twice before he was nine years old. When Chaplin was fourteen, his mother was committed to an asylum. As with Dickens, these tragedies were what fed the boy's passion for the escape of public performance. His teen years found him polishing what would become a major talent through comic pantomime in London music halls and on other stages. By nineteen, he was well known and signed on with the prestigious Fred Karno company, with which he travelled to America. Scouted very soon after arrival by agents of the burgeoning film industry, he was brought on by the Keystone Studios in 1914. Quickly he learned to direct, and his shorts with Mutual in the latter teens made him one of the most recognizable performers in the world. By 1919 his position was so secure that he was able to co-found United Artists and gain total artistic control over his now full-length features. *City Lights* (1931) fell securely in the middle of his great artistic period when he wrote, starred in, and directed *The Kid* (1921) and accomplished the same in *The Great Dictator* (1940). Chaplin's rise from obscurity to international acclaim as an artist and public figure can only be compared in the English-speaking world with a Shakespeare or a Dickens. It is simply breathtaking to behold, and especially now given the critical distance of a century.

Beyond this history and the place of *City Lights* in the arc of Chaplin's glorious train, the film also stands as an example of what only film can do. *A Farewell to Arms*, *To Kill a Mockingbird*, *A River Runs Through It*, and others succeed as novels *and* films. *City Lights* could only be a film, and a silent film. It is a work one must experience to understand what all the noise is about. I have a good friend, a Chestertonian and a genius in his own arena, who often says that his first introduction to a high-level aesthetic awakening came when he saw *City Lights*. The very last scene brought him to tears. The great novelist and film critic James Agee must have had a similar reaction, calling the concluding moment of the film, "the greatest piece of acting and the highest moment in movies." *City Lights* offers all the best that Chaplin had to offer—pure slapstick, consummate pantomime, perfect timing and physical coordination, and a touch of the common bawdy blended with pathos and grace in a package of aesthetic beauty.

*City Lights* is a small film in many regards, an intimate character sketch with minimal plot and a simple background, documenting life in the lower classes. A poor tramp in a big city falls in love with a blind flower girl who thinks him a rich gentleman. The Tramp manages to find money to pay for her eye surgery though it lands him in prison. Once out, he meets her briefly in a moment of mutual clarity. The plot might describe a nineteenth-century melodrama. The film's greatness is all about how it is performed and played upon screen.

In its execution, *City Lights* might be classified as an attempt at the kind of total art that Wagner aspired to achieve. Chaplin also composed the music for the film. In addition, he made it three years into the sound era. At the time, Chaplin considered sound film a passing fancy as the talkies seemed crass and lacking in the visual, narrative sophistication of the best of the earlier films. Silence was universal, whereas the talkies divided the industry into stylized bites like the Tower of Babel. Chaplin first began writing and producing *City Lights* in 1928, with the delay in release largely due to his perfectionist tendencies. It cost him more than two million dollars, an absolute fortune in that day, but he had as high an artistic ideal as his main character had a love for the blind girl. The handwriting may have been on the wall for silent films, but Chaplin saw that form as purer than what was coming, and he saw that the path of resistance to the herd served his comprehensive artistic conception far greater than had he capitulated to immediate market and industry demands.

Consider with this context that America was in a precarious economic circumstance in 1931. Many of the more successful films of the early 1930s were escapist fare, like the Berkeley musicals which followed *City Lights* two years later, *42nd Street* and *Golddiggers of 1933*. Unemployment averaged over 14% during the Great Depression, peaking at nearly 25% in 1933. The rich man in *City Lights* enters the action with the intention of committing suicide. Chaplin in typical counterintuitive fashion guessed correctly that the hard times would welcome a bit of nostalgia. He also understood that his Tramp character would have special appeal to the men who would stand in bread lines and come home with head low from drudgery to equally dismal domestic circumstances.

While celebrating the uniqueness of the Chaplin masterpiece, one might additionally consider the anomalies of the story. *City Lights* is a film in which the main character seems intent on going to jail, not escaping it. Likewise, the hero in *City Lights* does not "get the girl" in the end—to think he does is to mistake all the cues and diminish the luminous conclusion. Likewise, the girl's desire to "find the right guy" runs terribly and literally afoul. The wise become fools and the fools wise. Also, the American Dream is the butt of many jokes in the film, and this while the majority of those in the audience would have longed for the American Dream more than anything else.

Like all enduring works, the arc of *City Lights* runs a direct line from the first frames to the last. Even in scenes of pure physical comedy—the long trajectory gags, the subtle and not so subtle facial reactions, the pratfalls, the contrasting planes of action—the dominant themes remain. They can be described through a set of polarities: public versus private, rich versus poor, prominence versus insignificance, old versus young, blindness versus vision, carnality versus transcendence. And one might recast these in such a way as to suggest the film is an illustration of the beatitudes:

*Blessed are the poor in spirit: for theirs is the kingdom of heaven.*
*Blessed are the meek: for they shall possess the land.*
*Blessed are they that mourn: for they shall be comforted.*
*Blessed are they that hunger and thirst after justice: for they shall have their fill.*
*Blessed are the merciful: for they shall obtain mercy.*
*Blessed are the clean of heart: for they shall see God.*
*Blessed are the peacemakers: for they shall be called children of God.*
*Blessed are they that suffer persecution for justice' sake: for theirs is the kingdom of heaven.*
*Blessed are ye when they shall revile you, and persecute you, and speak all that is evil against you, untruly…*

An examination of the opening scene of *City Lights* reveals this entire thematic structure. We are at an intersection in a large city, judging from the congestion all around. A crowd has gathered for the unveiling of a large offering of public art. The mayor and a socialite, both oozing self-importance, offer speeches, their words the sounds of a kazoo, Chaplin's cue that this will be a silent movie—get that out of the way… The moment comes and the sheet is pulled away, and the hidden revealed, Chaplin asleep upon a hilarious parody of neo-classic public sculpture. The crowd is in an uproar, but the Tramp is undaunted. He begins to perform to the crowd without apparent intent. As he tries to escape the statue, a stone broad sword held by one of the figures, some effete Roman noble lounging while holding it in a provocative angle, pierces the Tramp's pants, offering an unmistakable commentary on the whole event. The Tramp tries and manages to escape only to commit a series of other faux pas. He sits on the face and then steps on the crotch of the lounging noble, ties his shoe sitting on the hand of a second statue, a figure holding up a hand in the fashion of Caesar, then places his nose on that statue's thumb while tipping his hat and pointing to the crowd. It is a tour-de-force opening salvo.

The scene is as memorable in the film as the famous concluding image. In trademark fashion, the great Chaplin defines the territory and reminds viewers of what is ahead. But there is a statement of theme here as well. We have no use for the pomp of civic duty and public virtue. We despise imitative art as much as Howard Roark in Ayn Rand's *Fountainhead.* Beyond that, we acknowledge that under the surface of modern efficiency exists an underground culture of the poor and destitute. The hero is a tramp after all, and a sympathetic one—he sees and knows the deal, whether he can articulate the premises well or not. The fat mayor and prim socialite are the faux characters, as are the police, embodied in Keystone Cops fashion in the opening scene as a blustering captain demanding the Tramp leave this "sacred space." It is not sacred space, of course, but a pompous display of civic madness. The monument deserves the treatment the Tramp gives it. Throughout the film, those who pretend authority and importance will be made the butt of jokes, from the rich benefactor who enters the Tramp's life to make promises only to take them back, to the butlers and waiters who serve the wealthy and put on airs, to those who mask carnal passions by elegant dances and costuming, to the police who patrol the streets and eventually haul the Tramp off to prison, to the bosses and foremen and promoters, all the complicit who make the system work. The more connected to the system, the dimmer the soul.

Only a genius like Chaplin could pull off so much information with so minimal means, and we cannot miss his sophisticated understanding of both human nature and corporate corruption throughout *City Lights.* The scene that immediately follows the opening salvo at the monument continues the motif of sophisticated art as sham, though here the shamming is not the principal concern, but the hidden reality behind modernity. A sidewalk on another street finds the Trump casually strolling as if a Wodehouse character, despite his outward looks. He pauses in front of a shop. In the window is a full-sized nude statue, one imagines it in a tacky gold leaf. The Tramp considers as though a connoisseur, surveying the thing with feigned professionalism though his eyes furtively stroll up and down the curves. He plays for an imaginary audience again, extending the gaff by stepping back to get a different perspective. When he steps back, we, the real audience, note a large grate on the sidewalk. It opens and the Tramp backs onto the edge oblivious to his parallel. He steps forward, then back, and repeats it with a different step. When he finally recognizes his peril, he acts again, this time scolding a worker who happens onto the platform. The platform ascends to sidewalk level, revealing that the worker is large, much larger than the Tramp who feigns courtesy and makes a quick escape.

This scene sets up a couple of motifs to follow. The first is the visual gag of what is behind the Tramp that he does not see. This will be repeated over again throughout the film, often to great comic purpose, until the final scene when the motif flips and Chaplin appears behind the once blind girl who will then learn for herself how to see things front to back. Also, the statue introduces the contrast between empty carnality and true love; Chaplin first beholds the blind girl in the following scene.

This latter contrast between carnality and true love hearkens back to the classic work most similar to both the method and content of Chaplin's art, and that is Cervantes' *Don Quixote*. Repeatedly in the Cervantes classic, the hero's high aspirations will be contrasted with the base desires of those around him. Famously, Don Quixote's first sally as knight errant will takes him to a local inn where…

> *The girls were looking at him and straining their eyes to make out the features which the clumsy visor obscured, but when they heard themselves called maidens, a thing so much out of their line, they could not restrain their laughter, which made Don Quixote wax indignant, and say, "Modesty becomes the fair, and moreover laughter that has little cause is great silliness; this, however, I say not to pain or anger you, for my desire is none other than to serve you."*

Cervantes plays the joke throughout. When overhearing romantic chatter from two women in residence at a duke's estate, Don Quixote will let out a feigned sneeze to alert them of his presence and so not wound their modesty, as he sees it; the reader does not, for the girls have other aspirations than to be courted in the conventional style.

One line of humor that Chaplin runs throughout the film and that underscores this same point regards effeminacy. Several times the Tramp will find himself in an awkward physical position in relation to his rich benefactor—while escaping the rope on the river's edge, sharing a bed, et al. Toward the conclusion, when trying to earn quick cash by agreeing to box a match against a local, the Tramp attempts to win the mercy of his opponent through overly friendly gestures in the locker room that lead the man to go behind a curtain to change out of his trousers. There is a serious point here, as in *Don Quixote* and other Chaplin films, and that is the effects of poverty on manliness and marriageability, a theme one finds in the other great comics of the era as well, Buster Keaton and Harold Lloyd. Unless the hero can obtain some level of financial stability, he will be left caressing the bed post. One imagines this truth found ready understanding with the immigrant men who had moved to the cities for mostly factory work and who formed so large a proportion of the early silent audience.

The next key scene has Chaplin first encountering his Dulcinea, the blind flower girl, an antiquated character for us, but like the balloon man a recognizable figure in Chaplin's day. The girl sits on a ledge with an iron fence behind her, the type defining the front yards of the rich in New York, Boston, or Chicago. This choice of location seems merely a wise business decision but comes to suggest more as the story unfolds, when we discover the girl dreams not only of renewed sight but of a traditional benefactor as well. Her position in front of the fence matches with many other scenes in which physical and social restraints plague her; in the last scene we understand that the true restraints have been in her mind. The Tramp first takes note of her as he walks along because of her beauty, only to discover her blindness when she cannot find a coin that drops on the ground. This discovery produces in him an expression of delight. He imagines in this instant that all might come together in a bundle, his desire for a woman, and a beautiful woman at that, and his escape from the critical scrutiny of his own inadequacies. Complicating the equation, while triggering the arc of the story, is that the girl thinks he has come from one of the limousines parked along the street. The Tramp, the proven performer we have seen, readily adopts the role of rich man to achieve the goal of his quest.

The impossibility of the situation is apparent to the audience, though the characters are all caught in self-delusion. Chaplin tips this off when the girl, unaware that her "rich suitor" has feigned leaving and taken a seat nearby from which he can watch her, tosses the water from her container into his face and shirt front. The momentarily dismayed hero exits quickly. We understand the implication for the rest of their affair.

If the thematic structure is not apparent at this point, Chaplin will reinforce it in the following sequence that introduces the third main character, the rich benefactor. It is on a walkway beside the river, a setting no doubt perhaps familiar to Chaplin from his early days walking along the Thames in London. Chaplin descends the stairs to the find the man drunk, disheveled, and about to commit suicide via a rope around his neck attached to a stone, props which Chaplin will use to create one of the most memorable comic bits in his films. When the Tramp realizes the man's intention, he slips into a role again, "Tomorrow the birds will sing…" He punctuates the sweet cliché with a dramatic flourish, slicing the air overhead with his hand. The man is not impressed and continues his mission, and the two end up in the water several times with the rope and rock their nemesis until rescued by the appearance of a cop, this one time to save the day. The two men leave the waterfront as newfound friends. The rich man in his drunken state can see the human soul of his friendly mediator, not the social role of the tramp.

Again the themes emerge one upon the other. The rich man is the poor man and the poor the rich, at least in heart and character. The rich man is blind to the Tramp's plight. The Tramp sees past the class disparity to a brother in need. The comic embraces of the two suggest a parody of the human fellowship the Tramp so ardently desires. The city which presented itself in such pomp and sophistication in the opening scene is revealed for what it is with its dark underbelly of despair and shame.

The plot likewise unfolds logically scene after scene, brilliant gag after gag, to the climactic resolution. The Tramp has been visiting the girl who with her grandmother takes it as a courtship. He has paid her rent with his meagre earnings as a street cleaner; this, of course, beginning his own redemption—work is a virtue after all, especially when it allows the support of others. He has suffered the indignities of his rags and foolish demeanor, and the humiliation of being the on and off friend of the rich man, off when seen for what he is and not through the man's drunken haze. He has been knocked cold in a boxing match, his only opportunity to achieve his quest despite his obvious inadequacy for the sport; one thinks of Coleridge joining the Light Dragoons. Meanwhile, the girl believes he is a knight of the first order, a rich man with courtesy and respect in the eyes of the world. After all, he came out of a fancy car in the first scene, although he really did not. The Tramp knows at heart that it is all a charade, a comic jest of providence. But he loves her, and that is no jest. His sacrifices and his humility are real.

The girl can now see, the result of a miracle eye cure from some mythic physician the Tramp reads about in the newspaper, a bit of satire even here, though rendered poignant by the girl's and the Tramps' desperation. The Tramp obtained the money for the operation from the rich man when drunk. Once sober, the rich man will and does, of course, want the Tramp to rot in prison as result. No matter, the girl gets the gift and now owns a shop with her grandmother, seemingly on the same street where the Tramp saw the nude statue. The same boys are there, too, mocking him even more now that his baggy clothes are in complete tatters. The clothes seem to have shrunk on the poor man as well, a metonym for what prison life brought to him.

The Tramp appears before her shop. His back is turned as he shoos away the mocking boys. The girl laughs at his antics with another associate, both oblivious to who he really is. We see, however, and in an instant, all is clear, the tragedy and comedy of the whole situation, and our situation by extension. All our romantic notions, our foolish big dreams, the secret hopes for our ship to come in as Ralph Kramden would say—all are about to be crushed. You could not paint a more pathetic figure than the Tramp framed in the girl's window and thus seen with perfect clarity in the cold light of day; this moment before the window, held for only a few seconds, breaks your heart. Then something magical happens. The Tramp turns and recognizes his beloved. Even when she takes him in and laughs, he retains his gaze. She is beautiful, and she can see. That is all that matters. If he had opportunity in life to do one noble act, one act of pure charity, all might be redeemed. And here it is, the gift has been received; she had the operation with the money he obtained on his own and gave her, and now she can see. But, of course, she doesn't see yet, not really, and that is the heartbreaking reality of life in our collapsed world. Dulcinea is common after all, like all the rest.

But wait, the title card might read. When the girl steps outside to give the Tramp a coin, she touches his hand, and the music shifts to strings in a minor key. She realizes who he is. She touches her head in unbelief and acute anguish. "You can see then?" He points to his eyes. "Yes, I can see." That last shot, one of the most famous in all early film and the one Agee singled out, is Chaplin's expressive, joyful, tentative gaze. Yes, love can conquer all, can redeem all. The hero's love has made of the common girl the maiden he sought. And her recognition, her own expression of love in so trying a moment, has made him the knight he aspired to be.

These final declarations of *City Lights* reverse the curse. Quasimodo is not left desolate to haunt the towers of the great cathedral. Don Quixote is not left in such despair that he denies his books and his noble deeds and dies a broken man surrounded by friends who realize too late what he really was. Dante is not left in the Dark Wood. Followers of Chaplin films from those early decades of the twentieth century knew who the Tramp really represented. It was only within the confining world of his film narratives that the truth tended to be missed. But not in *City Lights*. We have a witness, and of all ironies, the witness is not a maiden born of purity, the smell of the woods, and sparkle of the morning sun on the river. She proves as common as our hero; yet she is transformed by him into an image worthy of a holy icon.

When the penitent Dante finally meets his Beatrice midway through *The Purgatorio*, she will implore, "Yes, look at me! Yes, I am Beatrice!" The reward for all the pilgrim poet's efforts is this first beckoning of sanctified love incarnate—Behold! He may look for he has been made clean, and he has passed the best that earthly pleasure can offer, the new Eden atop the lofty mountain of purgation. And Beatrice will lead him upward to something greater still, for the end of his romance is not a bride of flesh and blood. Dante will receive the beatific vision. His last guide, the old saint of Clairvaux, will provide final direction where to find his greater desires satisfied, "In order that thou mayst complete perfectly thy journey, for which end prayer and holy love sent me, fly with thine eyes through this garden." What lies beyond? Behold, "bound up with love in one volume, that which is dispersed in leaves through the universe; substance and accidents and their modes fused together, as it were, in such wise, that that of which I speak is one simple light."

The conclusion of *City Lights* depends for its power on this transfiguration at the end. Mortal becomes immortal in the humbled vision of knight and maiden. Darkness is overwhelmed with sudden light; yet both the characters know at heart that their illumination will be as momentary as Moses' glowing face which remained veiled so that the people of God would be spared the sorrow of seeing its diminishing glory. Chaplin's instincts were never better than in his decision to end the film with the Tramp's enraptured gaze.

One is forced into analogies and other devices to articulate the effect, but such is the case in Scripture as well. Dark to light. Demonic to angelic. Base to pure. Folly to wisdom. The Whore of Babylon versus the Virgin most pure. For Beauty to be described requires metaphoric contrast, and the end of *City Lights* offers us a decidedly Christian rendition of the Beautiful.

The modern world has largely lost the ability to invent such things. More recent trends have been to invert the concept, to play that the base and ugly can be perceived as beautiful, a backhanded way to discredit the thing itself. That is, the modern impulse is to insert a bone through a woman's nose, capture the moment on a camera, and insist the aesthetic effect is a matter of taste. Christianity brought Western culture the beatific vision and the honor-bound knights questing to obtain it. It brought us Beatrice, and even Dulcinea. Modernity, on the other hand, has brought us what Henry Adams saw at the Paris World's Fair in 1900, the dynamo as emblem of power—power to name and unname, to make and to unmake, without conscience and without beauty.

Some time back Joseph Campbell wrote a book called *The Hero of a Thousand Faces,*[16] largely a popularized version of Sir James Frazier's *Golden Bough*. The book might as well have been titled *The God of a Thousand Faces,* as Campbell argues that all religions emanate from common roots, that the dying god of Christianity is just another take on the universal dying god motif found in many other religions; in other words, a way to place into imaginative form the universal hope that humankind can someday overcome death, that the inevitable rhythms of nature which all conclude beneath the soil can be redesigned to our everlasting favor. It seemed a compelling idea at the time finding its way into the popular consciousness through the *Star Wars* series, George Lucas being a Campbell disciple—

"Remember the Force, Luke." The Force. But if a Force, then whoever owns the Force owns God, one might surmise. Whoever controls the power of naming owns the thing named. The idea behind Campbell's thesis is Wittgenstein and Orwell and Stalin, all brought together at a common table.

Augustine reminded the world that evil can never create, just negate. Evil can only injure. The thousand faces of the popular god are the thousand faces of diabolism. Once the mask is peeled off, the revealed visage glares ahead with the same bloodlust—child sacrifice, the debasement of women, the corruption of sexuality, the defacing of the body, the countless blasphemies about the God who made the universe being housed in stone monoliths or clay statues.

Consider the ancient Egyptian myth of Isis and Osiris, a myth recast in numerous forms and perpetuated in modern society through the old fashion of masonic Bahomet worship. In the version of the myth told by Plutarch, the goddess Isis had twins, Seth and Osiris. In an inversion of the biblical account of Cain and Abel, Seth, the better twin, killed his brother Osiris, who was the most vicious of the gods. Then Seth cut the body of his evil twin into fourteen pieces and scattered them across the world. When his mother Isis heard, she went about recovering the body parts in order to reconstruct Osiris. However, she could only find thirteen of the pieces as a great fish had eaten Osiris' penis. So, Isis fashioned a penis of stone, a monolith, and made love to her son to resurrect him, which occurred as the stone phallus miraculously impregnated her. Isis would give birth to the sun god Horus, and the spires and monoliths across the globe of all the various cultists through the ages stand in cold tribute to the "miracle."

How one equates that pagan incarnation and resurrection myth with Bethlehem and Calvary and the empty garden tomb is a puzzle that amounts to understanding how a daisy and a razor might be compared, both described by words formed of five letters. There is nothing beautiful or inspirational about the Isis and Osiris myth; whereas Bethlehem and Calvary and the empty tomb continue to inspire song and poetry and lives of heroic charity. Bethlehem and Calvary and the empty tomb are the inspiration behind *City Lights*. They can be seen in the soft-focus haze that illumines the background behind the miraculous transfiguration of the Tramp and the humbled woman. He had no beauty that we should admire him, Isaiah says. Christ on the cross was mocked by those with blind minds; however, when he appeared to John on the Isle of Patmos, his head and hair were white like wool and his eyes like flames of fire. Mary was a common girl about to be quietly put away by her righteous Joseph. When John sees her in his Revelation, she is glorious like the Arc of God, a woman clothed with the sun, with the moon beneath her feet, and on her head a crown of twelve stars. All of that and much more is implied in that final moment of Chaplin's masterpiece.

Will the Tramp become a middle-class success as result of his heroic virtue? Of course not. But he achieves a sanctity in the end that is infinitely better. Will the girl make him over, break his spell as in *Beauty and the Beast*? No, she will undoubtedly go on to find a man more to her taste but whose heart bears some resemblance to her hero; she will keep the poor Tramp as an image on a shelf or in a book, a reminder of the unexpected mercy that made possible her security and domestic comfort. She will bear children and tell them the story in muted version of the kindly, harmless angel that providence sent her way on a day when she least expected.

This sober view takes us full circle to our initial reflections about the heaven we all desire. The purpose behind the romance in life or poetry or novels or film or song or all together is to enrich our understanding of the ineffable. All is grace. All is love. And we understand love by loving. It might be said that we fall in love by loving. So also, we see heaven most clearly only when looking into and through the eyes of our dearest to the home around so beatific a vision.

# 12
# SUNRISE

*Love is not love*
*Which alters when it alteration finds,*
*Or bends with the remover to remove:*
*O no! it is an ever-fixed mark*
*That looks on tempests and is never shaken.*
—Shakespeare, *Sonnet 116*

The previous discussion of Chaplin's *City Lights* described the storyline of that film as an American version of the German *kammerspielfilm*; that is, an intimate character sketch with minimal plot and a simple background documenting life in the lower classes. The poor tramp in a big city falls in love with a blind flower girl who thinks him a rich gentleman and whom he eventually saves. The film for this present discussion fits that model even more directly, F. W. Murnau's *Sunrise*. Country man is tempted by city woman only to come to his senses and return to the homestead. It is a universal tale, "of no place and every place" as the opening title card declares. The subtitle also gives the matter away, *Sunrise: the Story of Two Humans*. Just as *City Lights* might be underestimated because of its simple story and stock characters, so also might *Sunrise*. In both cases, such a judgment would be far off the mark.

F. W. Murnau was one of the geniuses of early film, both in his German career and his career in Hollywood after 1926. Four of his films—*Nosferatu* (1922), *The Last Laugh* (1924), *Sunrise* (1927), and *Tabu* (1931) stand near the top of any list of the greatest films of the twentieth century. The first, *Nosferatu*, birthed an entire genre and subcultural history. Upon his tragic death at age forty-two in a car accident, the industry bemoaned the loss of the many masterpieces that would certainly have come from his mature period.

A significant part of Murnau's gift was the ability to pull story material into larger conceptions about the mysteries of human relationship. *Sunrise* serves as example, a haunting study of temptation and redemption and the influence of marriage and family upon a community. Murnau adapted it from an ironic story by Hermann Sudermann called "The Excursion to Tilsit," which involves a rather boorish man plotting his wife's death to enable an affair but instead changing his mind and reconciling with her. The two are then caught in a storm during which the means for the man's escape in his original murder plot becomes the means for the wife's escape, while the storm takes the man's life. Murnau's parabolic retelling not only deepens the plot by adding more dimension to the main characters, it also broadens the conception to address larger geopolitical realities—especially, the threats the emerging world places upon marriage and family. To do so, Murnau, as did Borzage in *A Farewell to Arms*, scraps the anecdotal ending of the Sudermann story in favor of one more optimistic in which the events become liturgical, not materialist.

The easiest way to explain the liturgical qualities of the Murnau film is to place it into the context of his earlier efforts on a similar theme in his horror classic *Nosferatu*. Horror film and sacramental Christian film are opposite poles of the same scale, one playing out demonic influence and the other angelic or divine. Like the hundreds of monster movies that would follow, *Nosferatu* plays out the infiltration of the common world by demonic forces, specifically the shape of the Transylvanian vampire popularized by Bram Stoker in his 1897 novel *Dracula*. The invention of that nefarious character goes back further to folk legend and to the other book written during that Genevan storm that birthed Mary Shelley's *Frankenstein*, the short novel *The Vampyre* written by Byron's physician John Polidori. All follow a basic horror scheme—human folly leads to the violation of ancient taboo which leads to the infestation of the evil entity. Once among the living, the demon produces death as a contagion until the desperate band of survivors discovers the formula of exorcism potent enough to cast the spirit back into the bowels of hell where it belongs. In *Nosferatu*, that climactic event is the rising of the morning sun which finally exorcises the vampire; the mediator for that salvific act is the self-sacrificing heroine Ellen Hutter, who allows the creature to feast freely on her blood through the night to save her beloved husband Thomas and the rest of the community.

Though that earlier Murnau classic might seem distant in subject from *Sunrise*, the title hints a connection. The rising sun which spells the end of the vampire ends the 1927 romance as well. The design of the plot also bears resemblance. The temptress city woman plays the otherworldly part, one might say, in that she has cast a spell on the poor country man she sets upon while on vacation. As a result, the man deserts his wife and child and plunges into a life of debt and dissipation, the contagion, all of which leads to the spider woman encouraging him to drown the wife, sell the farm, and join her in the city. The child is not even a consideration in the scheme. The man follows that bait onto the lake with his simple-hearted bride only to wake up from his slumber in the nick of time, a dog and some distant church bells helping to accomplish that rescue. The man then spends the day winning back his wife's trust and affection. While on the trip back home across the waters, however, a storm breaks suddenly and capsizes their boat. The man makes it to shore, but he and the villagers are horrified to learn that the wife appears to have drowned. Amidst this the man is confronted by the city woman who believes he has accomplished the murder per her plan, but he turns and nearly strangles her instead, only to be saved from that additional crime when he hears the call from the maid that his beloved has been found safe. The city woman is expelled from the city, the man restored to wife and family, and the villagers engage in rejoicing. Straightforward parable about good triumphing over evil but within the larger frame of demonic infestation, exorcism, restoration. The characters remain unnamed throughout to underscore these ideas—The Man, The Wife, and the temptress Woman from the City.

The victim husband of *Sunrise* is, as said, not quite as boorish as the Suderman original, but thick-headed and impulsive still. He might be described as a simple, hard-working young man who loves his family, but his initial approval of the murder scheme suggests a moral vulnerability that made him an easy target. The wife, on the other hand, is a woman of true virtue and strength. She demonstrates feminine qualities of tenderness and compassion and repeatedly weeps for the tragedy she has been pulled toward, but this does not stop her from lovingly tending her baby after her husband has left to meet the city woman, and then lovingly covering him and gently stroking his brow the following morning. She is characterized as ever-nurturing, daily stooping to feed their baby chicks, tending to their dog, other animals, and her wayward husband. The wife is a character of pure goodness, just as the city woman is one of evil. We are never given a scene with her displaying a shadow of jealousy, anger, or resentment, as wronged as she is. Janet Gaynor working under Murnau's artful direction manages this performance without seeming artificial, and this is necessary as the wife must be a credible vessel of grace to reverse the curse and rescue husband, family, and larger community.

The vampire of *Nosferatu* becomes the *femme fatale* from the city, and it takes a divine display of charity to expel her and rid the home and the village of the contagion, and that charity emanates again from the saintliness of the woman of virtue, antithesis to the city woman. As mentioned, in *Sunrise* the actual trigger for the man waking up from the spell is the dog and the church bell in the distance; both sounds standing in, one might say, for the sacramentals of the church which are the effective vehicles to convey divine grace. In another sense, these sounds are analogs for the various fairytale means of the Gothic genre—garlic, stakes through the heart, silver bullets, and the like. Their power is rooted in the wife's love and devotion played throughout the story. Her love is the real antidote, and an antidote effective because behind it is the greater grace she models. The man awakens from the spell of the dark woman by the deeper magic of the woman of light.

The evil woman seems to have grown out of the soil of the city just as the saintly wife does the rural countryside. Murnau makes this evident in the opening sequence of the film which visualizes a helter skelter of people moving through the city amidst towering buildings and trains and ships running in all directions—the temptress woman never moves across the screen smoothly and calmly as do the locals. This opening montage sequence describes vacationers lingering at a resort, a woman in provocative display foregrounded as a man comes up to her to try his luck. Then follow giddy city-goers arriving by boat to a rural town, the city not content to stay within its own borders but sprawling, one might say. It is a portrait of artificial urban happiness created for license and self-absorption, the city thus contrasted with the farm; Murnau furthers the contrast with a crosscut that shows the back story of how happy the couple were in their early days before the city vacationers arrived—the man working the land behind an ox, pausing only to kiss his wife and embrace his child. License and self-indulgence versus work and family life. The villagers allowing the city to mix in with their common life might be identified as being complicit in the violation of taboo that leads to the dark consequence. The people of God are told repeatedly to be separate from the world.

The victims follow the call of the vampire to their demise in *Nosferatu*, and so in *Sunrise* when the husband is first introduced in the story, he is under the spell of the evil woman who beckons him by whistling outside his window. We cut to him sitting at his kitchen table, bread uneaten in front of him, head down. At her whistle, he turns to the window like a possessed man might. His eyes tell of the torment, but he cannot resist, at least not until the heroine, his demure and industrious wife, quickly enters the room to arrange the table for their meal. This furthers the initial contrast of indolence and sexuality versus industry and domesticity. The city woman has her hair styled and covered fashionably. She has applied lipstick and has had an old peasant woman buff her shoes. She smokes carelessly. Though the man knows his place is indeed at the homely table, each time the woman whistles outside he moves closer to the sound and further from where he belongs, his body movements much the same as we see in the victims in the earlier Murnau film lured to their death through the hypnotic powers of the vampire.

As the whistles persist, the man follows the temptress outside to the grief of the poor wife who has no idea how to break the spell. In the light of the moon, the spider woman entices her victim, suggesting the plot to drown the wife and move to the city. The more he fights this temptation, the more passionate her kisses, until under the moon the man enters her full embrace, the image not centered in the frame but to the left, a visual cue that he has slid off the path of the ordered life. This moment of capture is then crosscut to the wife alone tending to their child who has become distraught, a motif that will continue throughout the action. In true romantic fashion, nature knows what is up—the child, the animals, the sky, the sea, and finally the sun which rises at the end. The wife weeps bitterly as she offers the necessary comfort. Meanwhile, the evil woman continues to weave her spell describing mad images of late-night city dances, pleasures without end—the very substance of disordered love.

As the man skulks home late that night, he passes through shadows which stretch across the lonely landscape to his barn where he will store the reed bundle meant to allow his escape from the death now planned for the wife. This haunting sequence of the possessed man haunting the dark night would influence other directors working with their own Gothic materials like James Whale and Carl Dreyer. When the door to the barn is revealed, we get it at a canted angle in the seminal expressionist style of Robert Wiene's *Caligari.* However, the spell cast over the man and the land is not so binding in this story. An agency of providence has been set in motion through the wife's purity and love, for once in the barn the man is startled by a horse which nuzzles him from a hidden side and which seems to nudge the evil bundle of reeds he is carrying. It is a surprising and slightly comic incident that tips the viewer like the entrance of fools in Shakespeare to the fact that matters might not end so terribly after all. The man has an ally of which he is not yet aware.

We get more information about this in the subsequent scene where the wife leans lovingly over her husband now collapsed on his bed. She sees his muddy boots and knows what must be up, but she plays the Madonna and leans down upon him as mother and virgin bride. Murnau sets this up with the ringing of a church bell in the distance, the sound that will return to save him in his moment of truth.

When the man suggests to his wife the idea of a day together on the water, she is filled with childish delight and shares the good news with her maid and child. However, while Murnau reveals her in full frame moving about the home happily, he crosscuts the image to the man's hands reaching down to the reed bundle which will, he thinks, save him from the water that will take her. It is a device much like one Robert Bresson would employ in several films, particularly *Pickpocket* (1959), to suggest the separation of action from reason, the man's head from his hands. The spell cast over him has frozen his conscience and taken over his will much as in classical obsession or possession cases.

On the water, the husband and wife appear small compared to the forces of nature around them, making her seem especially vulnerable. The camera observes her from the front emphasizing her light heart and playful spirit, her eager desire that this day trip may break him out of whatever has taken hold. Meanwhile, he is shot from behind, head down, shoulders up and hunched like a walking dead man.

The dog knows something is up and breaks free from his rope back home, leaps the fence as Lassie might, and dives into the water to swim to the wife's rescue. She takes him into the boat and hopes the man will respond kindly, but instead he rows back and re-secures the dog. At this point, she realizes his intention and looks around in shock at the expanse of the water, the gulls flying off, and her husband's unresponsiveness. As he rises slowly and begins to hulk forward, she leans back folding her hands in the manner of prayer to implore mercy, and just then the church bell rings again. The man looks down into his hands and wakes up, the spell broken by this miraculous, soft intercession.

The music changes from tense to more natural though now accelerated as he rows madly back to shore to escape this damning situation. She runs and he pursues, and again something magical happens—a trolley car appears from nowhere. She gets on and he follows.

The appearance of the trolley in this rural setting signals that the whole enterprise has been part of a large fairytale. Not a cheerful rags-to-riches fairytale like *Cinderella*, but a dark tale like *Hansel and Gretel*, two children of a father under a wicked stepmother's spell left alone in a forest with a witch who likes cooking children in her oven. *Sunrise* is just such a dark fairytale, and like all of its kind it serves as cautionary tale. The urban invasion of the pastoral countryside and the humble home of the man and wife is a very real threat. The city is not content to stay in the city. Pristine landscapes and traditional values have come under a dark influence, and it will take a heroic effort of character and value preservation, alongside the just providence of God, to protect the community. This point has been evident from the start. The invader woman of the city does not only threaten the man. His ruination will also bring the collapse of wife and child and all who depend on them as anchor and hope for the future.

The trolley ride takes them from the quiet alpine setting to the center of the city through the magic of fairyland. The driver requests his fare—everyone in the city that the man and woman will meet wants to be paid. The man now beholds the city firsthand through the windows, this magic ride designed to reveal the source of the evil for what it is. His eyes begin to open. The buildings that swirl past are without character and densely packed. The streets are full of dust as people and horses and cars rush in all directions. In its own way, the scene is as disconcerting as the carriage ride in *Nosferatu* which takes Jonathan Harker to Count Dracula's castle. The trolley having come to a stop, the woman runs out and crosses a busy street heedless of the danger, the man hurrying to save her.

As he takes hold of his brokenhearted bride, the man gazes around at this horror show of urban activity which appears all around him. He gets her to the walk and finds safety for them in a restaurant, but not a quiet place with tables placed discreetly. This one has walls and doors with high and mirrored glass, and the couple seems woefully out of place, but here is where the second dramatic change will occur. As the woman sits crumpled, unable to recover herself, the man takes a piece of cake from a plate and offers it to her, a sacramental offer of bread, a small good thing. She looks up in surprise and hope and tentatively takes the cake from him and begins to eat, before breaking down again in tears. These tears are different, however, as she has caught sight of the deep remorse in his face.

When the two leave the restaurant, the story transforms into something much lighter. As they walk down the street, he pauses to buy her flowers. He makes continual efforts to comfort her, his expressions the opposite to his demeanor in the boat. Then a bell once again rings softly, but this time they both register its sound. The bell rings yet again, and Murnau crosscuts to a church. The wife looks kindly into her husband's eyes. The sound continues, drawing them both inside where a wedding is taking place. In the fashion of the sacramental style mentioned earlier, their participation as observers of the wedding becomes immediate. The music turns plaintive and sweet. The minister is presenting the words of promise to the groom, but also to our new man in a way that edges his remorse toward true repentance: "God is giving you in the holy bonds of matrimony, a trust. She is young… and inexperienced. Guide her and love her… keep and protect her from all harm." The wife is caught up in longing with the beauty of the ceremony, while his face reveals the deep grief prompting moral awakening. He breaks into tears and collapses into her lap. The camera holds the image of salvation for them both, the man weeping, the woman looking up to the front altar as though in gratitude. She leads him to the back where he collapses to his knees before her, "Forgive Me!" The sacrament is complete. The church bells ring again. The marriage is restored.

To expand this moment of restoration, Murnau offers one of the more memorable sequences in the film. The two walk down the stairs from the church as though the bride and groom and then into the street oblivious of the traffic, a matching scene to her almost suicide after the trolley ride; yet here the cars seem to pass through the couple, a clever feat of superimposition and other camera trickery. The street then becomes what they imagine it to be—a field of hay lit by the sun. They stop for a prolonged kiss only to awaken from the reverie in the center of an angry traffic jam, rude city drivers honking and yelling without heed to the miracle that has occurred.

What will follow is the feast and dance, but Murnau injects the celebration with larger thematic questions that address the underlying class implications of the story. Why had the woman from the city pursued the man after all? He does not come across as a very intriguing character beyond his healthy, large frame. For her the adventure can only be plausibly described as a demonic game. She looks down on the poor folk who house her, shows no concern for the man's wife and child, and completely misunderstands the effect she is having on the whole community. For her, these people do not matter. She has learned these attitudes from her city life—self-absorption, that life is to be played at, that only this world in its fleeting condition exists. Her bourgeois, materialist snobbery will be mirrored in the scenes following the wedding scene.

While the man is trimmed at a barber shop, a worldly urbanite sits beside his wife and makes flirtatious overtures. In fact, all who encounter the couple from this point on, usually in the context of some sale, demonstrate in their behavior that these two are only country folk, and as such to be observed with merriment and condescension. Yet, these attitudes all prove false when in a series of events to follow the husband proves himself superior to all the other men. The sequence culminates when he catches a piglet escaped from a carnival that has turned a party into chaos. By the end, the influence of the country couple begins to transform all these city-goers in the fashion of Mr. Deeds and Mr. Smith in the Capra films to follow in a few years.

The film's concluding sequence develops these ideas. The fate of the man and his wife, their restoration to purity, influences the lives of all around them. This, of course, is a negation of the modern urban notions of self-determination and personal choice. Actions have ripple effects. We are told in the first scenes how the affair between the woman of the city and the man troubled not only wife but child and mother and neighbors, the whole town. One cannot escape the larger consequences of human choice no matter how those choices are justified—the broken marriage does incalculable damage. As the man and his wife begin to sail home under the quiet stars, Murnau reminds us that the effects of dark transgressions are not easily dismissed. Purgation is still required. While the two sail blissfully past a celebratory party onshore and play at kiss me-kiss me not in the boat, a storm breaks all of a sudden, as suddenly as the horse nudged the man and as the dog broke loose and as the bells began to ring. Though divine mercy has provided relief through fortuitous providence, justice demands its due.

The storm attacks the city first. As the contagion began there, so must the vengeance. Murnau shifts back and forth through several frames from the scene in the boat with the wife sleeping against the chest of the restored hero to the city swept by rain and wind. Lightning streaks across the sky, and partiers scurry for shelter but are blown about like leaves. The carnival where the man had caught the pig and where the couple had shared a fine dinner is blown to tatters. And then the storm hits the boat, less destructive at first, but then intensely, and the man is left struggling to keep the boat from capsizing as his wife sleeps. Finally, she awakes in horror. Could this comedy end as tragedy? Yes, it very well could, as it does in the Sudermann original story. The husband heroically ties the reeds to his wife and hangs on as best he can until the boat capsizes and the storm carries all away. The last image is of their village in the distance before the lights go out.

Murnau adds an interesting touch in this storm sequence. When the man desperately tries to row to shore, his oars break, one at a time. At this his terrified wife collapses into his arms, and he is left with no right action but to comfort her. And his resolve to comfort her, to do nothing but love her, is what saves them both, a mirror of his situation at the start. Their restored mutual love is the means by which salvation will come, a love that engenders the further grace of God. If they are to be saved, it will not come by human effort, but by the same providence which nudged him into sanity early on.

The plot leaves hanging the fate of the poor wife, the storm passing from the two capsized lovers to their child crying back home, comforted futilely by the frantic maid. Then all goes calm, and the man makes it to shore. The moon appears again from behind the thick clouds to light the way. His first impulse once he pulls himself up the rocks is to call his beloved, the sound that of a doleful horn. She is nowhere to be seen, and he grows more frantic. Meanwhile, we are taken to the cause of it all, the woman from the city asleep in her bed, oblivious that there even was a storm. She wakes at the tumult of the townspeople outside her window and looks out to see what is happening. The movement of the villagers and their lanterns inform her that her work has been successful, at least so she believes.

In an era before easy camera movement, panning and tracking, and before depth of focus lenses, Murnau accomplishes a remarkable sense of motion across multiple planes through heavy shadowing and the breaking of images into parts. As the woman looks out at the rushing villagers, she observes them through multiple panes, each pane framing a distinct action. The suggestion is how the woman's devices have spun the complex web that has caught them all. When she inches away from the light to hide herself, she shrinks into the frame, the smallish, warped creature she really is. We get a similar device in the following sequence when the woman follows the villagers and perches on a tree branch to view the action, the screen again divided into three frames by the branch and the shadow it casts, again suggesting the poison she represents, and referencing back to the early images of the city with vehicles of all types competing with the rushing crowd for space in the frame.

The man leads the search party of small boats, leaning forward lantern in hand as he calls her name. This action cuts back several times to the reaction of the spider woman who, unfeeling, believes she has succeeded and that his actions are a ruse for her sake. But then Murnau reveals the hidden truth, as through the dark waters floats the wife, unconscious but carried safely above by the buoyancy of the bundle of reeds, the bed constructed by the husband to save his own life, but now saving hers instead. However, the man is led to think the opposite when a closeup of his face registers horror as sees portions of the reed bed float past his lifeboat followed by fragment of his wife's garment. The villagers remove their hats in mournful solidarity.

This all sets the stage for the final conflict. Just as the man must redeem himself through repentance and renewed charity, and just as the marriage vows once broken must be proclaimed again in the church, so also must the source of the evil be exorcised. The woman of the city still lives and believes she has triumphed.

The disconsolate husband enters his bedroom crossed by the shadows from the windowpanes. It is another reversal, this of the earlier scene when his poor wife entered to see him collapsed on the bed from his night of licentiousness. She was tender in that moment, the woman of virtue from the Proverbs. His heart, however, lacks that generous love she demonstrated. He skulks through the room with a posture suggesting dark matters, though grief is the cause this time. As he collapses on the bed, Murnau again provides the signal that redemption is at hand. The church bell rings out over the moonlit sky. One more action is necessary.

The woman from the city has arrived outside the house. She calls him and slinks around the corner expecting the usual response, but she does not get that response. The man slowly raises his head and forms two fists. As she comes to the door, he emerges in the frame a hulking shape, and she realizes the game is up and runs. While this is occurring, Murnau inserts a shot of men recovering his wife's body and hurrying her to the house. Unaware of this mercy, the man catches the city woman and begins to strangle her over a shadowy picket fence, but then Providence intervenes one last time. The old thrush whispers Smaug's vulnerability in the key instant, and the black arrow of Bard finds the target. The man is saved from a murder that would reissue the curse through a nick-of-time call from the maid that his wife has been found alive. He tosses the evil woman aside and hurries inside. As we have seen in other films discussed in this book, films all drawn out of the folds of the Christian tradition, the man is saved by the woman in the end. He accomplishes the heroic task but only through the mediation of feminine love and virtue. This is not the cavalry come to save the day; it is Christ of Calvary speaking the word to still the storm at the instant the disciples are certain death is imminent.

The woman lays on the bed hair down and beautiful, a match for Catherine on the hospital bed in the last scene of Borzage's film. And just so, the couple's lingering embrace puts on display the woman's rapturous face. She is the object of desire and adoration. She glances heavenward with a look of gratitude before the townspeople all press into the room and begin merriment and storytelling of how the damsel was rescued by an old seaman who knew to look in one last place where the current tended around the point.

The conclusion shows the loveliness of the mist-covered Bavarian landscape, and then finally the defeated spider woman carted off to exile in the city from which she came. The morning sun rises over the home in benediction.

Murnau was born in Prussia but loved Bavaria and created his professional surname from a Bavarian district he had visited on a bicycle trip. Plumpe was his birth surname. He loved the beautiful Bavarian land and admired the people of both types, poor and rich. Though the Sudermann original was set in Lithuania, Murnau had Bavaria in mind with his filmic capture. It seems safe to conclude that with his admiration for the people he likewise admired their deep-rooted Catholic faith, and that he recognized the forces of the emerging world that would threaten these old customs and values. We might now affirm a hundred years later that his fears were more than warranted. It should be taken as gift that Murnau left the world a beautiful portrait of that world that once was and which could perhaps still be restored. All can be restored after all, though only, we surmise, through the return of the maiden fair whose virtues restore to man his original purpose.

Janet Gaynor who plays The Woman was one of the best-known starlets of the period, an actress who embodied natural beauty and fragility on a scale comparable to her more famous Hollywood star predecessor Lillian Gish. She was the first recipient of the Academy Award for her performances in this film along with two others, Borzage's *Seventh Heaven* (1927) and *Street Angel* (1928). Her realization of the wife in *Sunrise* makes believable a character whose virtues might otherwise be dismissed as unworldly. With hair pinned back under a covering and face subdued and vulnerable, she captures the simplicity of the wife, and then with hair flowing over the pillow in the raptures around her awakening, she dazzles the man and the audience with an aura of sanctity. The Wife has become the Madonna, the Virgin Most Pure, the Byzantine Our Lady of Tenderness, the Mother most Beautiful, worthy of the *Salve Regina.*

# CONCLUSION

*There can be no profitable reflection without previous reading, or hearing... Nor will beginners or proficients come to true prayer without previous reflection.*

—The Cloud of Unknowing

The subject of this book has been that bittersweet aesthetic response felt so often while watching certain of our favorite films, an aesthetic response similar to the one famously described by William Wordsworth reviewing in the theater of his memory of a walking trip to the ruins of the lovely Tintern Abbey:

*...a sense sublime*
*Of something far more deeply interfused,*
*Whose dwelling is the light of setting suns,*
*And the round ocean and the living air,*
*And the blue sky, and in the mind of man;*
*A motion and a spirit, that impels*
*All thinking things, all objects of all thought,*
*And rolls through all things.*

God calls us through nature, through the instincts of our minds, and through direct revelation; and he calls us as well through the secret aches of our heart.

The trigger for this book was quite personal. Five or six times in my life, events left me riding a wave of grief that lacked words. What later fixed these experiences in my memory was how random they seemed. Why then and not when Betty died... My attempts at talking these questions through with others after the fact always seemed foolish and self-indulgent, a waste of breath. Tears were the only appropriate vehicles of expression. Then through my career as a college professor teaching literature and film, I found myself having parallel experiences in the glowing moments of certain films. Back in the days of reel-to-reel projection, these were easier to mask in the glowing darkness and clicking of the machine, or through the business of returning reels to their cannisters. Not so easy once we entered our one-push-button world.

This present labor has been something of a science experiment. To explain the reaction, I proposed a hypothesis, that behind the tears in the defined personal and aesthetic reactions was a crack deep within, a crack that opened with a precise cut of key. That key was cinematic beauty expressing truths about our humanity. So, I questioned what aspect of that humanity was exposed in its hiding place behind the crack in that very secret and very personal place. The answer seemed obvious, universal human longings, two to be exact—the desire for heaven, or permanency if you prefer, and the desire for pure love. Has the experiment proven successful? I believe so, but leave others to follow up on their own. Assuming it true for the sake of the argument, what is the merit of the findings? A deeper experience and understanding of the power of beauty in God's world and a deeper love for God himself. And a more decidedly orthodox approach to film very much needed in our present, confused times.

Novel as this subject and my approach may have seemed at first blush, with so many pages turned I hope these conjectures now merit deeper consideration. Against any accusations that may come suggesting I have indulged a long and tedious afternoon reverie, allow some back-story. Underneath this science experiment rests considerable research into the mechanics of how filmmakers over the years have approached divine subjects. Years ago, when in graduate school and recommended to do a study of how religious films work on a formal level, I identified a stylistic tendency in that arena and termed it the sacramental style.[17] The designation was a response to an argument made by the writer and director Paul Schrader who saw a similar formalistic tendency in his studies of three great, "religious" directors: Yasuhiro Ozu, Robert Bresson, and Carl Dreyer.[18] It seemed odd to me that only and particularly those three directors would share a stylistic trait grounded in the mechanics of a specific genre, religious film, so I applied Schrader's conclusions to a wider range of films across generations and geographies. What I discovered was a common, sacramental approach to filmmaking similar in method to what devotional writers like Ignatius Loyola taught their disciples as means to experience the presence of God during prayer and meditation.

A great many films evoke the divine presence not as a concept or symbol, but as an active agent in the plot. They do so by merging the ritualistic aspects of Christian liturgy with the private concerns of popular piety. Such "sacramental films" follow categorical principles of mystical contemplation: composing the space, applying the intellect, understanding, will, affections, and so on. The medium of film, like that of the devotional exercise, is displayed in fixed time periods, on a rotational basis, and with a regular sequence of participatory steps.[19] The structures of individual films in the set follow certain generic patterns as they address subjects and audiences which hold set conventional understandings, and they follow industry principles of display and participation. And through time the best of these films have become prominent as popular expressions of piety.

This sacramental style is remarkably fluid for filmmakers telling a story grounded in faith. Framed another way, less significant than the numbers or quality of Jesus films (Mel Gibson's 2004 film *The Passion of the Christ*) or of films telling stories of saints (Henry King's 1943 film *The Song of Bernadette*) is the number of films that employ the principles of Christian liturgy to tell religious stories. The Christian liturgy progresses from the liturgy of the Word to the liturgy of the Eucharist, and films as disparate as Carl Dreyer's *Ordet* (1955) and William Wyler's *Ben Hur* (1959) do the same. Both directors found it necessary to reshape their narrative style to convey the climactic incarnation, the eucharistic transformation of the world through the entrance of God into the kingdom of their fiction. In *Ordet,* backlight pouring through a parlor in which a dead woman is miraculously raised bathes all the characters in a white glow to convey the wonder of the moment; in *Ben Hur,* violins played in a minor key coupled with an angelic choir adorn the scene when a mother and daughter are miraculously cured of leprosy.

Whatever the established style within an individual film of this type, that style is transformed in a dramatic way when the miracle of transformation occurs—often in a complete reversal of the previous methods of the film. The pattern is very much aligned with how the miraculous transformation is signaled in liturgy; that is, a sudden change in pattern—the slow lifting of the elements with the ringing of bells that follow moments of stillness.

For example, in the climactic sequence of Rouben Mamoulian's *We Live Again* (1934), a young Russian nobleman Nekhludov, played by Fredric March, overcome with guilt at having debauched and then deserted a young peasant girl named Katusha, enters his private room and closes the door. At this cue, the previously straightforward narrative flow of the film comes to an abrupt halt. What follows is a montage of cinematic gestures, a prolonged search into Nekhludov's soul. March walks slowly across the room to a piano; he sits and begins to play a doleful hymn. The shot dissolves into the interior of a church during mass, and then back to Nekhludov whose head is lifted in emotion as he plays. He rises from the piano and moves toward a mantle, upon which the camera reveals an icon. The soundtrack continues the hymn the remorseful man played, which increases in volume and fullness the nearer he draws to the icon. With a gesture of despair, Nekhludov bows before the altar and asks God's forgiveness so that he might "live again."

There is the shift in narrative technique, a shift toward formalism that describes an underlying, concurrent narrative track—the spiritual. The unique spiritual montage of Nekhludov's conversion in *We Live Again*, which occurs within a frozen or static moment of the surface narrative, permits a complete reshuffling of character behavior and narrative pattern. The spiritual realm has broken through the physical and will now redeem it. Nekhludov will leave his chamber a new man, merciful and sacrificial and heroic. We are the spectators of this conversion; through a similar potent grace by virtue of our identification with Nekhludov and embrace of the film's dramatic resolution, we are changed, too.

In sacramental films God steps into the story and transforms the material to make it truly real. The event may be conveyed by character gesture as in Bresson's films, or by cinematic gesture from crosscuts to symbolic iconography, a slowing of the action, overlays of sound or music or many other means. Often the physical gesture is joined with the cinematic, for example in the long montage sequence in *A Farewell to Arms* or Roy Hobbs' slow trot around the bases in *The Natural.* However the miracle is conveyed, it requires a directorial sleight of hand to communicate this something special with the audience. The method for conveying the entrance of God from director to director or film to film is one of means.

Too many films employ such devices to start a list here, but once you see a film like *We Live Again* or Wyler' *Ben Hur* (1959) and watch the incarnational scenes, you will understand exactly the point. If those examples are too distant, consider *Chariots of Fire* with Eric Liddell running in slow motion around the track in his gold-medal 400-meter triumph and his voiceover, "God made me fast, and when I run, I feel his pleasure." The means of telling the story changes right there.

The sacramental method with its diversity of practice argues the remarkable ability for the Christian faith to adapt to changes in culture and artistic practice; and just so, the Christian faith has had a powerful impact on every sphere of art in the West. While many wings of the Church, particularly in the United States beginning in the twentieth century, caution against the potential dangers of film as a corrosive influence on society, films continue to be made that play out central theological truths and which are recognized as masterpieces of Christian art.

I include this side trip for context, but also because it offers a bridge to a last thought. Both artists and those who consume art are people who, like all people, long to experience the presence of God. Talking about matters of faith is simply not enough. Church is not enough.

To experience the presence of God on a common stage demands an escape from usual religious enclosures; that is, the chapel or shrine or private devotional space where we may sit each day with Bible or rosary in hand. It must be blended into the flow of our day-to-day experience. The romantic poets tended to locate these extraordinary encounters in pastoral settings, which is all good for those like Wordsworth who dwell in a paradise of lakes and rolling hills and who have the leisure for long walks and poetic reflections. The assembly line worker lives in another reality. And, in that reality he likely watches movies and welcomes those which bring him moments of clarity.

Good movies can edge us toward heaven and the love that wants us there. We need more good movies.

As suggested at the start of this book, a positive outcome from the labor of your reading may be that you turn to one of the films discussed and discover something new, and in the discovery feel yourself come newly alive, even if through recollection of a sad, long-buried memory. In this fallen world, birth is painful, but it always leads to joy.

Isn't it true that we often get the clearest sight of heaven and feel the richest depths of love in those secret places where we cry alone?

# NOTES

1 Clive Bell, *Art* (London: Chatto & Windus, 1914).
2 Leo Tolstoy, *What Is Art?* (London: Penguin Classics, 1995).
3 Dietrich Von Hildebrand, *Aesthetics*, vol. 1 (Steubenville, Ohio: The Hildebrand Project, 2016), 47.
4 André Bazin, *What Is Cinema?*, vol. 2, trans. Hugh Gray (Berkeley, University of California Press, 1967), esp. 47-48.
5 Brian Loan, "Does This Man Really Think the Holocaust Was a Big Joke?" *The Guardian*, January 29, 1999, *https://www.theguardian.com/culture/1999/jan/29/awardsandprizes*.
6 G. K. Chesterton, *Orthodoxy* (New York: Image Books, 1959), 60.
7 Von Hildebrand, *Aesthetics*, vol. 1, 71.
8 Ibid., 49.
9 Joseph Pearce, *The Quest for Shakespeare* (San Francisco: Ignatius Press, 2008).
10 Norman MacLean, *Young Men and Fire* (Chicago: University of Chicago Press, 1992), 84.
11 Judith Thurman, *The Life of Karen Blixen* (Harmondsworth: Penguin, 1984), 329.
12 Tolstoy, *What Is Art?*
13 Dorothy L. Sayers, *The Mind of the Maker* (San Francisco: Harper Collins, 1941), 103.
14 J. R. R. Tolkien, *The Letters of J. R. R. Tolkien*, ed. Humphrey Carpenter (New York: Houghton Mifflin, 1981).
15 Colin Wilson, *The Outsider* (New York: Houghton Mifflin, 1956).
16 Joseph Campbell, *The Hero of a Thousand Faces* (Princeton, NJ: Princeton University Press, 1972).
17 Peter Fraser, *Images of the Passion: the Sacramental Mode in Film* (Westport, CT: Praeger, 1998).
18 Paul Schrader, *The Transcendental Style in Film: Ozu, Bresson, Dreyer* (Berkeley: University of California Press, 1972).
19 Useful here is Louis Martz, *The Poetry of Meditation: a Study of English Religious Literature of the Seventeenth Century* (New Haven: Yale University Press), 1954.

# FILMOGRAPHY

The following abbreviations are used:

| | | | |
|---|---|---|---|
| *ad* | art designer | *m* | minutes |
| *aka* | also known as | *mu* | music |
| *bw* | black and white | *p* | producer |
| *c* | cinematographer | *pc* | production company |
| *col* | color | *pd* | production designer |
| *d* | director | *s* | story |
| *ed* | editor | *sc* | scriptwriter |

***Babette's Feast***
*Babettes gæstebud*
Denmark 1987 103m col
*p* Just Betzer, Bo Christensen *pc* Panorama Film International/Nordisk Film/Danish Film Institute *d, sc* Gabriel Axel *novel* Isak Dinesen [Karen Blixen] *c* Henning Kristiansen *mu* Per Nørgård *ed* Finn Henriksen *pd* Sven Wichmann *cast* Stéphane Audren (Babette Hersant), Jean Philippe Lafont (Achille Papin), Gudmar Wivesson (young Lorens Löwenhielm), Jarl Kulle (old Lorens Löwenhielm), Bibi Andersson (Swedish lady-in-waiting), Hanne Stensgaard (young Filippa), Bodil Kjer (old Filippa), Vibeke Hastrup (young Martine), Birgitte Federspiel (old Martine).

***Brief Encounter***
United Kingdom 1945 86m bw
*p* Noël Coward, Anthony Havelock-Allan, Ronald Neame *pc* Eagle-Lion Distributors *d* David Lean *sc* Noël Coward, Anthony Havelock-Allan, David Lean, Ronald Neame *c* Robert Krasker *mu* Sergei Rachmaninoff *ed* Jack Harris *ad* Lawrence P. Williams *cast* Celia Johnson (Laura Jesson), Trevor Howard (Alec Harvey), Stanley Holloway (Albert Godby), Joyce

Carey (Myrtle Bagot), Cyril Raymond (Fred Jesson), Everley Gregg (Dolly Messiter).

***City Lights***

United States 1931 87m bw

*p* Charlie Chaplin *pc* United Artists *d* Charlie Chaplin *sc* Charlie Chaplin *c* Roland Totheroh, Gordon Pollock *mu* Charlie Chaplin *ed* Charlie Chaplin, Willard Nico *pd* Henry Clive *ad* Charles D. Hall *cast* Charlie Chaplin (Tramp), Virginia Cherrill (Blind Girl), Florence Lee (Grandmother), Harry Myers (Millionaire).

***A Farewell to Arms***

United States 1932 88m bw

*p* Edward A. Blatt, Benjamin Glazer *pc* Paramount Pictures *d* Frank Borzage *sc* Benjamin Glazer, Oliver H. P. Garrett *c* Charles Lang *mu* Milan Order *ed* Otho Lovering, George Nichols Jr. *ad* Roland Anderson, Hans Dreier *cast* Helen Hayes (Catherine), Gary Cooper (Frederic), Adolphe Menjou (Rinaldi), Mary Philips (Ferguson), Jack La Rue (Priest).

***To Kill a Mockingbird***

United States 1962 129m bw

*p* Alan J. Pakula *pc* Brentwood Productions, Pakula-Mulligan *d* Robert Mulligan *sc* Horton Foote *c* Russell Harlan *mu* Elmer Bernstein *ed* Aaron Stell *cast* Gregory Peck (Atticus Fitch), Mary Badham (Scout), Phillip Alford (Jem), John Megna (Dill), Frank Overton (Sheriff Tate), Brock Peters (Tom Robinson), James Anderson (Bob Ewell), Robert Duvall (Boo Radley).

***Life Is Beautiful***

*La vita è bella*

Italy 1997 116m col

*p* Gianluigi Braschi *pc* Melampo Cinematografica, Cecchi Gori Tiger Cinematografica *d* Roberto Benigni *sc* Vincenzo Cerami, Roberto Benigni *c* Tonino Delli Colli *mu* Nicola Piovani *ed* Simona Paggi *pd* Danilo Donati *ad* Danilo Donati *cast* Roberto Benigni (Guido), Nicoletta Braschi (Dora), Giorgio Cantarini (Giosué), Giustino Durano (Eliseo), Sergio Bini Bustric (Ferruccio), Horst Bucholz (Dr. Lessing).

***The Natural***

United States 1984 138m col

*p* Mark Johnson *pc* Delphi II Productions *d* Barry Levinson *sc* Roger Towne, Phil Dusenberry *c* Caleb Deschanel *mu* Randy Newman *ed* Stu Linder *pd* Mel Bourne, Angelo Graham *cast* Robert Redford (Roy Hobbs), Robert Duvall (Max Mercy), Glenn Close (Iris Gaines), Kim Basinger (Memo Paris), Wilford Brimley (Pop Fisher), Richard Farnsworth (Red), George Wilkosz (Bobby Savoy).

***Onegin***

British and American 1999 106m col

*p* Simon Bosanquet, Ileen Maisel, Ralph Fiennes *pc* Rysher Entertainment, Starz!, CanWest Global Television Network *d* Martha Fiennes *sc* Peter Ettedgui, Michael Ignatieff *c* Remi Adefarasin *mu* Magnus Fiennes *ed* Jim Clark *pd* Jim Clay *ad* Chris Saegers, Vera Zelinskaya *cast* Ralph Fiennes (Onegin), Liv Tyler (Tatyana), Toby Stephens (Lenski), Lena Headey (Olga).

***A River Runs through It***

United States 1992 123m col

*p* Jake Eberts, Robert Redford, Patrick Markey *pc* Columbia Pictures, Guild Film Distribution (in UK) *d* Robert Redford *sc* Richard Friedenberg *c* Phillippe Rousselot *mu* Mark Isham *ed* Robert Estrin, Lynzee Klingman *pd* Jon Hutman *ad* Walter P. Martishius *cast* Craig Sheffer (Norman Maclean), Brad Pitt (Paul Maclean), Tom Skerritt (Rev. Maclean), Brenda Blethyn (Mrs. Maclean), Emily Lloyd (Jessie Burns).

***Rocky***

United States 1976 120m col

*P* Irwin Winkler, Robert Chartoff *pc* Chartoff-Winkler Productions *d* John G. Avildsen *sc* Sylvester Stallone *c* James Crabe *mu* Bill Conti *ed* Richard Halsey, Scott Conrad *pd* William J. Cassidy *ad* James H. Spencer *cast* Sylvester Stallone (Rocky Balboa), Talia Shire (Adrian), Burt Young (Paulie), Carl Weathers (Apollo Creed), Burgess Meredith (Mickey).

***The Searchers***

United States 1956 119m col

*p* Marian C. Cooper, Patrick Ford *pc* C. V. Whitney Pictures *d* John Ford *sc* Frank S. Nugent *c* Winton C. Hoch *mu* Max Steiner *ed* Jack Murray *ad* James Basevi, Frank Hotaling *cast* John Wayne (Ethan Edwards), Jeffrey Hunter (Martin Pawley), Vera Miles (Laurie Jorgensen), Ward Bond (Samuel Clayton), Natalie Wood (Debbie Edwards).

***Sunrise***

United States 1927 95m bw

*p* William Fox *pc* William Fox Studio *d* F. W. Murnau *sc* Carl Mayer *c* Charles Rosher, Karl Struss *mu* Hugo Riesenfeld, Emö Rapée *ed* Harold D. Shuster *ad* Rochus Gliese *cast* George O'Brien (The Man), Janet Gaynor (The Woman), Margaret Livingston (The Woman from the City), Bodil Rosing (The Maid).